IBSEN THE NORWEGIAN

IBSEN
The Norwegian

A Revaluation
by

M. C. BRADBROOK Litt.D.

PROFESSOR OF ENGLISH AND FELLOW OF
GIRTON COLLEGE IN THE UNIVERSITY OF CAMBRIDGE

New Edition

1966

Chatto & Windus

LONDON

Published by
Chatto & Windus Ltd.
42 William IV Street
London W.C.2

★

Clarke, Irwin & Co. Ltd.
Toronto

First Published 1946
Second Impression 1948
New Edition 1966

Printed in Great Britain
by Butler & Tanner Ltd, Frome and London

Contents

v

Acknowledgements

My thanks are due to The Hogarth Press for permission to quote from Mrs. Woolf, *The Death of the Moth and other Essays* : to Mr. T. S. Eliot and Messrs. Faber and Faber for permission to quote from *Four Quartets* and *Murder in the Cathedral* : to Messrs. Hodder and Stoughton for permission to quote from the translation of Ibsen's *Correspondence* published by them : to the American publishers, Messrs. W. W. Norton and Co., Inc., for permission to quote from Professor Koht's *Life of Ibsen*, from the edition issued in this country by Messrs. George Allen and Unwin: and to Thom Gunn and Messrs. Faber & Faber Ltd. for permission to quote the extract from his poem *Human Condition* from the volume entitled 'The Sense of Movement.'

Preface

THE purpose of this book is to restore Ibsen to his background, and thereby to reveal his true proportions. A better scholar than myself is needed for the task, but I hope that what I have written will help the common reader to understand an artist whose greatness has of recent years been increasingly appreciated but who is as yet somewhat scantily furnished with critical apparatus in English, and much in need of retranslation.

A picture book of Norway is still, in my opinion, the best Companion of Ibsen Studies. The reader should banish from his mind the whiskered old gentleman of the portraits, and call up instead the tides foaming round the skerries, or the little wooden houses in the mountains.

In quoting Ibsen's poetry I have cited the Norse in footnotes to give readers, if possible, some glimpse of its power ; but I thought it would be tedious to continue to quote a language unfamiliar to many, and have therefore omitted the originals of the prose passages. This does not imply that the prose loses any less in translations than the verse. I have translated "du" as "thou," in spite of its oddity to the Southern ear, since the usage is so significant. Except in the proper names Haakon and Kierkegaard, where the modern form is familiar to Englishmen, I have retained the old form of long a.

My thanks are due to my Norwegian friends, especially to Professor A. H. Winsnes, of the University of Oslo, for his kindness in reading the manuscript. The book was written during the intervals of war work in London, where many of Ibsen's countrymen shared the night watches with me, and on one occasion rescued me and my manuscript from the débris of a flying bomb. To those friendships I would dedicate this book, and especially, remembering those of the Kongelige Norske Marine, "til de beste."

M. C. BRADBROOK

Cambridge
August, 1946

IBSEN'S LIFE

1828			Born at Skien (20th March)
1844	aged	16	Leaves for Grimstad
1850	„	22	Leaves for Oslo. *Cataline, The Warrior's Barrow*
1851	„	23	Theatrical post in Bergen
1855	„	27	*Lady Inger*
1856	„	28	*The Feast at Solhaug*
1857	„	29	Theatrical post in Oslo—*The Vikings at Helgeland*
1858	„	30	Married (30th June) to Susannah Thoresen
1860	„	32	*On the Vidda, Terje Vigen*
1862	„	34	*Love's Comedy*
1863	„	35	*Kingmaking*
1864	„	36	Prussian–Danish War. Leaves for Rome
1866	„	38	*Brand*
1867	„	39	*Peer Gynt*
1868	„	40	Goes to Germany
1869	„	41	*The League of Youth*
1871	„	43	*Poems*
1873	„	45	*Emperor and Galilean*
1877	„	49	*Pillars of Society*
1878	„	50	Returns to Rome
1879	„	51	*A Doll's House*
1881	„	53	*Ghosts*
1882	„	54	*An Enemy of the People*
1884	„	56	*The Wild Duck*
1885	„	57	Visits Norway, returns to Germany
1886	„	58	*Rosmersholm*
1888	„	60	*The Sea Woman*

IBSEN'S LIFE

1890	aged	62	*Hedda Gabler*
1891	,,	63	Returns to Norway
1892	,,	64	*Bygmester Solness*
1894	,,	66	*Little Eyolf*
1896	,,	68	*John Gabriel Borkman*
1899	,,	71	*When we Dead Wake*
1900	,,	72	Seizure and collapse
1906	,,	78	Death (23rd May)

References in the Notes

Koht. THE LIFE OF IBSEN by Halvdan Koht. 2 vols, *Allen & Unwin*, 1931 (trans. of IBSEN, ET DIKTERLIV, 1929)

Corr. THE CORRESPONDENCE OF HENRIK IBSEN, translation edited by Mary Morison. *Hodder and Stoughton*, 1905

Chapter One

THE MAKING OF AN ARTIST

*Ibsen and the Ibsenites—Ibsen and the Norwegians
The Norse Inheritance*

"HE who would know me fully must know Norway."
So said Ibsen to a German who could not understand
Rosmersholm. Yet no great writer of that age has been
more cut off from his background and his own early history
than Ibsen. Singleminded devotion to his art fashioned a life
that, because it is largely uneventful, has been thought without
significance. His command of the theatrical[1] has given him
an international fame which is partly independent of the language of the plays, and this has made for wide recognition;
but imperfect knowledge. The feeblest translation could not
disguise that *A Doll's House* is structurally well-built and as
good theatre as *Charley's Aunt*; this is not altogether a happy
thing for Ibsen. A knowledge of his country, his background,
above all of his writings in the original, brings up as many
unsuspected colours as the cleaning of an Old Master. The
work is not only seen more clearly, but it is seen to be
different.

After the age of Ibsenism, which in England was the 'nine-
ties, came the reaction. "The drama, like the symphony,
does not teach or prove anything," wrote Synge. "Analysts
with their problems and teachers with their systems, are soon
as old-fashioned as the pharmacopœia of Galen—look at Ibsen

---

[1] Purely as a *theatrical*, as distinct from a *dramatic*, artist Ibsen offers the
actors more than Shakespeare. Hjalmer Ekdal or Hedda Gabler as parts
are more fully within the scope of a great actor than Falstaff or Cleopatra,
where the interpretation must always be partial. And though an actor may
prefer that his reach should exceed his grasp, and attack Hamlet rather than
achieve Rosmer, the theatregoer will derive a satisfaction from having
absorbed Ibsen in a performance which no performance of Shakespeare can
give.

and the Germans . . ." [1] and, with Huxley and Tindall and Bastien-Lepage, Ibsen's name was anathema among " companions of the Cheshire Cheese ".

This reaction is long since dead, but it is still too common to think of Ibsen as the Restoration thought of Shakespeare —indubitably a genius but how deplorably outmoded ! To see Ibsen merely as the precursor of Shaw and Brieux when he was also the precursor of Strindberg and Tchekov [2] is to retain at this late date the false perspective of his contemporary critics and admirers. His contemporaries found the true Ibsen in the plays of his middle period, and slurred or depreciated his other work. Hence a generation which abandoned naturalism most unwisely abandoned Ibsen, forgetting that his early reputation was based on a very small proportion of his work, although the conflicts which he provoked made it the duty of all true Ibsenites to cherish, modify, and utilize even his least doctrinaire productions.

In so far as Ibsen has a constant theme, it is the destructive power of genius. The biological determinism of *Ghosts* and *The Wild Duck*, the social preoccupations of *A Doll's House* and *Rosmersholm* do not mean that Ibsen's true place is in the army headed by John Stuart Mill and brought up by H. G. Wells. Of course, Ibsen had twinges of the hopes and fears which were common to his age, but his more constant preoccupation was the spiritual conflict which is born of the vitality of Brand, Nora or Solness, which brings dislocation and ruin on the life of their nearest. The troll in all of them gives them power, and denies them peace. All, like Emily Brontë's Heathcliff, are born to dominate and blindly to destroy even where they most love, as much by their own superabundant power as by untoward circumstance. If Ibsen saw mankind as the victim of fate, it was not merely as the potential victim of syphilis, like Osvald, but as the inheritor of " the thousand natural shocks that flesh is heir to ".

---

[1] Preface to *The Tinker's Wedding*, 1907. Synge forgot that Ibsen wrote *Peer Gynt*.

[2] " You know Ibsen is my favourite author," Tchekov to A. S. Vishnevsky (*Letters*, tr. Garnett, p. 495).

What a towering mount of sin
Rises from one small word : To be [1]

Original sin has seldom had a more Calvinistic interpretation
than it received in Brand.

Ibsen's most naturalistic studies transcend the science of his
day. Dr. Wangel's treatment of his wife's neurosis might
have been learnt from a psycho-analyst but would have been
somewhat in advance of the textbook therapy of the time.[2]
Gunhild Borkman would fit into a case book that should also
include D. H. Lawrence's Mrs. Morel. Nor was Ibsen
averse from drawing from the life. But the root of his
greatest plays remains a poetic unity, a single vision, even
when they are not written in verse. *Bygmester Solness* was
crystallized out in eight lines of verse ; a vision of " the burnt-
out pair ", Solness and Aline, sitting in the rubble of his
" burnt-out faith " and her " burnt-out joy " cannot be
reduced to a tract on the New Woman with some observa-
tions on the power of natural hypnosis.

Two facts need not only to be accepted but to be grasped
before Ibsen can be fully known : that he was, all his life, a
poet and a Norwegian, that he wrote in a language not generally known or easy to translate and set his plays in the least
known country of Western Europe. Professor Halvdan
Koht, the greatest living student of Ibsen, opens his *Life* with
these words :

Henrik Ibsen was a poet.
This would seem self-evident ; yet it may be useful and even
necessary to establish the fact definitely from the beginning.
Too many have attempted to make him a thinker or a philosopher, a social critic or social reformer. He himself was fully
conscious that his genius was that of the creative artist and he
desired to be not merely an artist first and foremost, but wholly
and in all things an artist. He once expressed in a single word

---

[1] *Hvilket skyldberg der sig højner*
fra det lille ord : at leve.

[2] Halvdan Koht says revivals of this play in the 'twenties were much more
successful than the original production (*Life*, II, p. 248), and more recent
revivals in this country have also succeeded.

the meaning of poetic art. To a young man who himself dreamed of becoming a poet, he said : " To be a poet is to *see*." [1]

Koht goes on to describe Ibsen's struggle to *see*, to embody in images, and how it necessarily involved a measure of self-dissection. The experience which is embodied must have been directly " lived through " and creation was not easy for Ibsen. He was acutely, " even morbidly ", sensitive to the movement of life about him. " Almost unconsciously he sensed the thoughts that were in the air." [2] But he did not build his plays spontaneously upon this sensitive appreciation. He struggled to transmute it. There was distinct separation of the man who suffered and the mind which created.

The legendary picture of Ibsen does not suggest delicate and vulnerable sensibility. Formidable, irascible Herr Doktor Ibsen in his frock coat and silk hat, keeping even his family shut out from his writing, regulating his life by clockwork, jealously collecting decorations and orders, protecting his copyright and balancing his investments, is not a poetic figure. And yet his latest works most clearly of all

> were born of spiritual need and principally bear witness to the drama within his own soul. . . . Many things which at that time seemed involved and enigmatic find a direct and natural explanation when one sees them in relation to the spiritual life of Ibsen himself. [3]

His early life supplies the clue. The cruel struggle of his first thirty-eight years, embittered by poverty, contempt and crossed friendship, had hardened the stony mask upon him. Not even Kierkegaard masked himself more completely than Ibsen. The thoughts that still in old age " went through him like a spear " were of his early failures ; and in that early story, far more important than his relations to any individual were his relations to his country. He had longed to speak for Norway, he had thought in terms of Norway's freedom, and hoped to become a great national poet. His rejection by

[1] Koht, I, p. 1.
[2] See Ibsen's own words, below, p. 12, and ch. 3, p.82.
[3] Koht, II, p. 310.

his own people led to a kind of spiritual excision, and yet always, and most distinctively in the last plays, the tone and temper are Norwegian.

2

Ibsen's early life was restricted and unhappy. He was the child of a man who had sunk from being a prominent figure in his little town to poverty and seclusion. The family hid their necessities in a small farm outside Skien, which was all that remained to them of a comfortable property ; their rich relations turned aside. At sixteen Ibsen was sent to an even smaller coastal town as an apothecary's apprentice. He spent six years in wretched isolation, despised by the local gentry and in his turn despising and lampooning them, living in a small boisterous circle of callow literary youths. His family was henceforth cut out of his life. He neither corresponded with nor recognized any of them, save Hedvig, his little sister. The ruthlessness which cut him off from his family was later to cut him off from Norway, and for the same reason—wounded pride and the need for detachment.

In Oslo and later in Bergen, Ibsen struggled desperately to live by his pen. In Oslo he often went hungry. Later, at Bergen, he earned about 30s. a week as " Theatre Director " at Olë Bull's National Theatre. As a producer he was too shy and timid to correct the actors, and he seldom opened his mouth at rehearsals ; but he worked conscientiously as stage manager, plotting out the sets and arranging for the scenery and properties. Except *The Feast at Solhoug*, his own plays, were all complete failures, and he had the mortification of seeing others, especially his friend Bjørnson, winning rapid success and fame. In controversy he was crushingly snubbed by the local celebrities.

Yet Ibsen was not a recluse. He enjoyed students' parties and the liveliness of mental swordplay. He had more than one ardent love affair before he wedded Susannah Thoresen, and he had a cause to fight for. All his dramas are based on the medieval past, when Norway had been free, the time to which the patriots looked back for inspiration. One is based on ballad style, another on the sagas—in somewhat Danish and doctored form.[1] The mere existence of the National Theatre was part of the struggle. The strong propagandist bent in all his early work is not generally recognized but it culminates in the early masterpiece *Kingmaking*, a play which means far more to Norwegians than to the outside world.[2] Ibsen's main work in these years, however, was not dramatic but poetic. He was a popular " festival poet ", and poured out exhortations to his countrymen on national politics, which were well-received but unremunerative.

All his hard work and enthusiasm came to nothing, however. The theatre in Oslo, to which he transferred, failed, and was obliged to close. He was refused a Poet's Stipend. The first play in which he found himself, *Love's Comedy*, raised a storm by its views on marriage, and the clergy. At this time too Ibsen was filled with shame and rage that after pro-testations of sympathy, Norway did not join Denmark in resisting the Prussian attack on Slesvig-Holsteen. The satirical poem *Brother In Need* is the strongest expression of Ibsen's feelings, but they also found an outlet in *Brand*. This was the deepest disappointment of Ibsen's life. He never forgave Norway. The experience must have been comparable to that which so many young writers felt in this country between 1934 and 1939.

Throughout these lean years Ibsen was slowly falling into debt, and his little family was almost destitute. He had a nervous illness, and in spite of the success of *Kingmaking*, the strain had told on him so severely that he could go on no longer. With £90 granted by the Storthing, and some private subscriptions collected by friends, he left the country. A short time afterwards, his poor household goods were seized and sold by a creditor. He passed through Berlin as the population were riding the gun carriages and spitting into the mouths of the cannon captured from the Danes at Dybböl, and went on to Rome, where after two years of the deepest

[1] See below, p. 23.   [2] See below, p. 23.

poverty—his wife and child went short of bread in these hard times—he won success and security with *Brand*.

But by now he was thirty-eight years old. He had developed slowly, partly because such was his temperament, partly because there was so much spadework to be done on the language before he could establish something of a dramatic tradition.[1]

That Ibsen " went into exile "—his own phrase—at thirty-six is no proof that he cared little for Norway : rather it is proof how much he cared. The exile is the most significant fact in his emotional life, and the early writings help to an understanding of this fact. He went out into the desert, as the scapegoat bearing the failure of his people : for the artist must bear the burden of seeing the implications which his countrymen do not see. And he may have felt personal shame as well, for, whilst some of his friends volunteered for the Danish army, Ibsen lacked the courage for that final step and disguised his timidity, as many have since done, by the plea that an artist fights with his own weapons. His defiance ;

I'll be delighted to sink you the Ark ! [2]

his denunciation ;

We are sailing with a corpse in the cargo ! [3]

and the vehemence of his letters, which show that even after twenty years the sting of his rejection remained, are proof that his disappointment had nearly killed him.[4] The wounded wild-duck flew south only after it had tried time and time again to build a nest in Norway.

[1] See below, pp. 21–22.
[2] *Jeg laegger med lyst torpédo under Arken !*
[3] *Jeg tror vi sejler med et lig i lasten !*
From *Til min ven revolutions-taleren* and *Et rimbrev* respectively.
[4] " I often wonder how you can endure life up there ! Life there as it now appears to me has something unspeakably wearing about it : it wears the soul out of one, wears the strength out of one's will." (*Corr.*, p. 139.)
" [When] I sailed up the fjord I literally felt my breast tighten with a sense of oppression and faintness. The same thing was true of my stay there : I was no longer myself among all those cold and uncomprehending Norwegian eyes in the windows and the streets." (*Corr.*, p. 386).

His wounds were deep in proportion to the strength of his feelings, and had he loved Norway less he would have found it possible either to forget or to return. As a Scottish or Welsh mountaineer may chafe against the narrow and intolerant codes and the hard life of his birthplace, but, if he leaves it, will be haunted by memory and drawn home in spite of himself, so Ibsen never ceased to think of Norway. He associated with Scandinavians, he devoured the Norwegian newspapers, and he never acclimatized himself anywhere else. From Rome to Naples, to Dresden, to Munich, he wandered about for twenty-seven years, living in hired rooms. He had no public life and gave himself up entirely to his work, maintaining a close seclusion, though he avidly collected honours, trophies, decorations, degrees, any public mark of success. "They were a sort of weapon to him and could even serve as a defence of his spiritual freedom." [1] They proved that if his countrymen did not recognize him, " there was a world elsewhere ". Exile from a small country like Norway is more bitter than exile from one great nation to another. The Englishman in France, the Frenchman in England, is less cut off from his natural roots because his national background is more readily appreciated, and its influence can be felt abroad. Exile for Ibsen was not like exile for Byron.

Ibsen had to make a hard choice ; and he chose to be solitary in order to be great. He was shy, but too susceptible to his friends' views ; he could not speak out freely in their presence, even as he could not speak out to the actors in Bergen. He wrote to Brandes :

> Friends are an expensive luxury, and if a man's entire capital is invested in a calling and a mission in life, he cannot afford to keep them. The costliness of keeping friends does not lie in what one does for them, but in what, out of consideration for them, one refrains from doing. [2]

Ibsen's sensitive and receptive mind was made more sensitive by his personal timidity. He admitted that he was

[1] Koht, II, p. 77.   [2] Corr., p. 183.

physically a coward. When the wealthy Herr Holst caught the penniless student making love to his daughter Rikke, and rushed forward, "green with rage", the lover ingloriously fled. Ibsen was afraid of dying of cholera, or being killed in a street accident, or bitten by a mad dog, and he refused to take part in any risky sport ! But if he were not brave " face to face ", he had the desperate courage to lead a life of loneliness in order to be free. At a distance he could endure the unmeasured rage which his satire drew down upon him. He could even enjoy it, and hit back—on paper. In person, he grew only less and less communicative.

Another reason why Ibsen exiled himself was what he called his " longsightedness ". His sensitiveness to immediate impressions meant that their first effect was overwhelming and he needed time to reflect.

> We human beings in the spiritual sense are long-sighted creatures ; we see most clearly at a distance ; the details confuse ; we must get away from what we desire to judge ; one describes summer best in winter. [1]

Later, in an address to Norwegian students, Ibsen suggested that this process of longsightedness belongs especially to the artists.[2] It was after he left Norway, and after he ceased consciously to concentrate on Norwegian national aspirations that he wrote his most intensely Norwegian plays, *Brand*, *Peer Gynt*, *The League of Youth*, and *Pillars of Society*. The first two depend on the atmosphere and quality of life in the North, the last two are faithful pictures of life in Skien and Grimstad, studies in small-town politics, filled with portraits drawn from life.[3] Distance alone gave Ibsen the power to *see*.

Yet gradually a change came over Ibsen's work, and the price of exile was heavy. *Love's Comedy*, *Peer Gynt*, and *The League of Youth* stand alone as genuine examples of comedy.

[1] ibid., p. 193. [2] Koht, II, pp. 8–9.
[3] e.g. Ibsen's father appears in *The League of Youth* as Daniel Heire, Stensgård owes something to Ibsen himself, something to Vinje but more to the poet's friend and benefactor Bjørnson who was head of the " Young Party," the nationalist left-wing in Norway.

Not merely are they conceived as comedy; there is a Shake-spearean richness and fecundity about them, which, except perhaps in *An Enemy of the People*, does not appear again. The lively wit, the gay rhymes, the happy-go-lucky caprices of the plot disappear, as the poetry itself disappears, to be replaced by a strict and finely tempered prose—not the experimental style of the earlier plays but a style precise and tooled. The gain was immense; but something was lost. The world gained a dramatist: Norway lost a poet.

Gone, too, was the gay and Bohemian Ibsen, who drank swaggering toasts to the confusion of his enemies. The ascetic Ibsen emerges, in the plays (" Brand is myself in my best moments ") and in life—the Ibsen who drove away callers with an " Arbeitsruhe ! ", who had made his choice to sacrifice friends and home. He had foreshadowed this renunciation in the poem *On the Vidda*, and in *Love's Comedy* : but the effects were not fully seen till later. What the immola-tion cost him, he did not himself realize till the very end of his life.

Yet through the plays there begins to run what a psycholo-gist might call the Iphigeneia motif—the murder of the child. Alf, Olaf, Osvald, Hedvig, are victims whose signifi-cance is only fully seen in relation to Solness's babies, little Eyolf and the "child" of Irene and Rubek. What had been murdered was the childlike part of himself—the fresh unreflecting sensuous vitality which feeds the poet. Spon-taneity had been deliberately sacrificed for the benefits of dis-cipline and control because Ibsen felt that this was necessary for the good of his work. Ibsen, like Rubek, had become " first and foremost an artist ". The craving for immortality, which he had felt from his youth, when he said to Hedvig : " I wish to see all things clearly. And then I wish to die," had taken possession of him. He was completely sure of himself. When his countrymen criticized *Peer Gynt* he uttered the superb remark : " It IS poetry ; and if it is not, then it will be. The conception of poetry in our country shall be made to conform to the book."[1] His sacrifice had

[1] *Corr.*, p. 145.

turned him into a fighter, and in *An Enemy of the People* he came to terms with Norway—the terms of a genius who is confident enough to accept and provoke an attack.

In ten years the majority will, possibly, occupy the point which Dr. Stockmann held at the public meeting. But during these ten years the doctor will not have been standing still. He will still be at least ten years ahead of the majority.[1]

His anger with Norway gave him the power of the lash : his eighteen years' struggle as a writer drove him to study stifled and oppressed lives. The plays of his middle period were built out of his own experience, transmuted into impersonal form. He himself acknowledged that Norway's greatest gift to him had been the gift of suffering and ironically he thanked her for it.[2] Ibsen was built " to see much and to suffer more " : suffering made of him an artist. His early works are full of undirected and unharnessed energy and the history of his development is one of concentration, the growth of perspective and of the power to select. Pressure of circumstance converted the naïvely enthusiastic and wildly iconoclastic country boy into the ascetic and coldly skilful surgeon of abuses. Because his sufferings and disillusion set him above the issues of the day, Ibsen could write both for an age and for all time, as Dante could write both for Florence and for all Christendom. It is indeed with Dante that he can be most readily compared in stern self-devotion and uncompromising exposure of deceit and weakness. Some words which Yeats wrote of the transforming power of that suffering which the Fates imposed on Dante might have been written of Ibsen ; though Yeats himself looked upon Ibsen as a kind of Antichrist and would not have allowed him even the name of artist.

. . . They have but one purpose, to bring their chosen man to the greatest obstacle he may confront without despair. They contrived Dante's banishment and snatched away his Beatrice, and thrust Villon into the arms of harlots and sent him to gather

[1] ibid., p. 370. [2] In the poem for the millenary celebrations of 1872.

cronies at the foot of the gallows, that Dante and Villon might
through passion become conjoint to their buried selves, turn all
to Mask and Image, and so be phantoms in their own eyes. . . .
Had not Dante and Villon understood that their fate wrecked
what life could not rebuild, had they lacked their Vision of Evil,
had they cherished any species of optimism, they could but have
found a false beauty, or some momentary instinctive beauty, and
suffered no change at all, or but changed as do the wild creatures,
or from devil well to devil sick, and so round the clock.[1]

Ibsen's life was built on tragic isolation : he became more
and more sealed off from his friends.   There was no dramatic
catastrophe.   But his letters gradually became drier and fewer,
his speeches colder, his silences deeper.   In the end there was
a gulf between him and his wife.   "They are two lonely
people," wrote his mother-in-law.   "Each lives absolutely
for himself."   It seems that the house of Borkman, in atmosphere at least, is not entirely without relation to the house of
Ibsen, although we have Ibsen's word, at an earlier stage, that
"My private relations I have never made the direct subject
of any poetical work." [2]

He added that in his earlier life these relations were unimportant, but that in such poems as The Eider-Duck and
Mind's-Might, which were autobiographical, the suffering was
there "because I have been co-responsible in a time which
buried a glorious thought amid song and feasting".   This
glorious thought was the "great kingly thought" of national
unity.

Ibsen went on to say :

All that I have written this last ten years [i.e. since his exile]
I have mentally lived through.   But no poet lives through anything isolated.   What he lives through, all his countrymen live
through together with him.   For if that were not so, what would
establish the bridge of understanding between the producing and
the receiving mind ?

[1] "The Trembling of the Veil", Autobiographies (Macmillan, 1926),
pp. 338–9.
[2] Speech to the Norwegian Students, 1874 : Speeches and New Letters, tr.
A. Kildal (Frank Palmer, 1911), pp. 49–50.

It must be allowed that while the poet cannot be completely isolated in his generation, he himself is at the growing point of the general consciousness : he evokes and clarifies what is but half-known. By his exile, Ibsen purchased the power to *see* both himself and others. He was, as he had wished to be, quite alone. He did not even maintain any contact with the theatre. The production of his plays did not interest him. His interest in politics waned. In 1868 he wrote the poem *To my friend, the Revolutionary Orator,* in which he declared that revolution was not enough, and proclaimed his belief in anarchism ! By 1870–1 the reaction had taken such hold of him that he wrote to Brandes :

> Now there is absolutely no reasonable necessity for the individual to be a citizen. On the contrary, the state is the curse of the individual. . . . The waiter makes the best soldier. . . . The state must be abolished ! In that revolution I will take part. Undermine the idea of the state ; make willingness and spiritual kinship the only essentials in the case of a union—and you have the beginning of a liberty that is of some value. . . .[1]
>
> I have never really had any firm belief in solidarity ; in fact I have accepted it only as a kind of traditional dogma. If one had the courage to throw it overboard altogether, it is possible that one would be rid of the ballast which weighs down one's personality most heavily. *There are actually moments when the whole history of the world appears to me like one great shipwreck, and the only important thing seems to be to save oneself.*[2]

If Ibsen were blatantly astray with the rest of his generation on the subject of the decay of nationalism, the last sentence shows that it was no facile optimism which led him on.

It was despair which had turned him away from his nationalist hopes. It was his sense of the Great Disappointment which drove him to introspection and the study of individuals.

> It is often evident to me that there is nothing left in our country for anyone gifted with mind and heart to do, but to retreat like the wounded deer into the thicket, to die in solitude and silence.

[1] *Corr.,* p. 208.   [2] ibid., p. 218.

The best thing that could befall our country would be a great national disaster. If we could not stand that, we should have no right to exist.[1]

Yet although the strength and independence of his characters—all that stamps them dramatic and pits them one against the other—was the creation of his own genius, that genius itself sprang from a race of whom it has been said : "Three million different Norwegians, three million different opinions". His experience of the Great Disappointment is behind the choice which confronts his characters—sacrifice or self-fulfilment. Each of them, in his several way, has to make this choice, and each demonstrates the same conclusion —that an exacted sacrifice is deadly, but a chosen sacrifice is required to attain the full stature of Man. The negative and positive poles of choice, Nietzsche's distinction between "freedom from . . ." and "freedom to . . ." each exert their force upon the protagonist, but Nora, Mrs. Alving, Osvald, Hjalmer, Hedvig, Rosmer, Rebekke, Ellida, Hedda, Løvborg, all attain peace when they freely choose the hard alternative— or they fail, in so far as they are incapable of choosing it.

Ibsen's exaltation of sacrifice springs from his intense pleasure in the exercise of the Will.[2] He himself felt that to enjoy anything was almost a challenge to forgo it. The pleasure of exercising the will in this way is not that of domination but of self-conquest, yet this ascetic pleasure can become as reckless as self-indulgence, and is indeed but self-indulgence in an inverted form.

The exercise of the will enabled Ibsen to maintain incomparable control over his own artistic powers. He gave up painting and literary criticism to concentrate on the drama— though he had been deeply interested in both. He gradually narrowed and controlled his dramatic method and then, equally surprisingly, began to expand its range again. He seemed able to modify his style into completely new forms,

[1] *Corr.*, p. 155.
[2] The two thinkers who influenced Ibsen most profoundly, Kierkegaard and Schopenhauer, both stressed the doctrine of the Will. See below, p. 43 and p. 66.

as a tadpole changes into a frog.   After *Brand* he changed even
the character of his handwriting from a spidery scrawl to a
firm neat heavy backhand.   He gave up poetry with the
finality and decision of a convert abjuring strong drink.[1]
When he returned to Norway in 1891, at the age of sixty-
three, he found the younger generation, in the person of Knut
Hamsun, knocking at the door.   On a famous occasion,
Hamsun lectured to an audience, which included Ibsen, on the
inadequacy of the elder writers.   Out of his own stung vanity,
Ibsen drew material for *Bygmester Solness*.   His last words
were inspired by the spirit of contradiction.   " Look ! " said
Fru Ibsen as he lay in seeming coma, " the Doktor is getting
better."   Ibsen opened his fierce blue eyes and glared.   " Not
at all ! " (*Tvert imod !*) he said severely.

Sometimes his advocacy of " the egotistical-sublime " may
shock by its ruthlessness.   He wrote to Brandes, his disciple
and self-styled " standard bearer "—and a good example of
Kierkegaard's dictum that to have disciples is the greatest
misfortune that can befall anyone :

> What I chiefly desire for you is a genuine full-blooded
> egoism which shall force you for a time to regard what concerns
> yourself as the only thing of any consequence, and everything
> else as non-existent.   Now, don't take this wish as evidence of
> something brutal in my nature !   There is no way in which you
> can benefit society more than by coining the metal you have in
> yourself.[2]

Ibsen's readiness to sacrifice all for his art was the last
infirmity of a very noble mind, and his exile is devoid of outward event.   There is nothing to record.   At the end of his
life he repented and saw this asceticism not as sacrifice but as

---

[1] In 1891 he wrote to Hedvig on the occasion of a public hall being opened
in Skien : " Had the festival taken place some years ago I should, if I had
been told of it, have written a song or poem and sent it home. . . . But I
no longer write poems and songs of the kind required.   So this is out of
the question."   (*Corr.*, p. 438.)   Evidently no exceptions could be made !
Ibsen thought that poetry was *harmful* to the drama, perhaps because he himself wrote more readily in verse.   See below, p. 23, note 3.

[2] *Corr.*, p. 218.

murder. With unsparing strength he wrote his palinode and retracted *coram populo*. But his pride was reprieved. The public did not understand, and thought he was writing about the New Morality, Hypnotism and Revolting Daughters, the burning topics of the hour.

The return to Norway had coincided with the revival of Ibsen the poet. Although the last plays were written in prose, it is more and more clearly seen to be the prose of a poet. Such passages as Borkman's hymn to the spirits of the mine, or Allmers's account of his vision in the mountains are closer to Ibsen's earlier work than to the writing of his middle age. The revival of the poet was, however, the eclipse of the dramatist. These last plays have little feeling for the stage ; their cloudy and stormy beauty must lose something in the presentation. But something, too, has been fully released which before was present only by implication. It is in these later plays that the early poem *Et Vers* is most openly justified.

> To live is to war with the troll
> In the caverns of heart and of skull.
> To write poetry—that is to hold
> Doom-session upon the soul.[1]

The struggle is again seen in the old terms—the terms of *Love's Comedy* and *Brand*. With the return to Norway, the old themes had been called up in Ibsen's mind.

His work falls therefore into four main groups : first, the 'prentice work, the making of the artist, which grew out of his struggle with Norway : then the early work of the exile, poetry and satire, still closely connected with his former experiences. Then the great series of plays from *A Doll's House* to *Hedda Gabler*, in which the poet and the Norwegian, suppressed but intensely active, worked underground like Ibsen's Miner but are clearly discernible none the less. These plays, it may be said, were written *at* the Norwegians. Finally come the visionary plays.

[1] *At leve er—krig med trolde*
I hjertets og hjernens hvaelv.
At digte—det er at holde
dommedag over sig selv.

But before considering the development of the work, it is necessary to recall what was implied by being a Norwegian between 1828 and 1900—what it meant to live in Norway and write in the Norwegian language.

3

A country long enough to stretch from Gibraltar to the Shetlands, with a coastline that, pulled out straight, would go half-way round the Equator; where the long journey by water was the shortest route from one closed valley to the next, where the tiny towns squeezed between the fjell and the fjord. A people strong but without natural wealth; a language unfingered by sophistication and impressively simple; beauty, poverty and isolation. Such was the Norway of Ibsen's youth. Compared with almost every other country of Western Europe it was virgin land, virgin of history, yet fortified with the traditions of ancient glory.

This stern and inaccessible country at the beginning of the nineteenth century was inhabited by just over a million people : seamen, fishers, farmers.[1] There was no nobility, for Norway had never known feudalism ; the tradition of local independence was strong. Shut in the narrow dales, each small community dealt with its own problems and lived largely unto itself. The "great kingly thought" of a united Norway was coming to birth in a country which, though politically unified, had hitherto seen local sentiment predominate over national feeling. Although the country was moving towards national independence—the Declaration of Eidsvoll being regarded by all Norwegians as the foundation of their sovereignty [2]—and although the development of

[1] Even now its population is barely equal to that of Wales, i.e. *circa* 3,000,000.

[2] In 1814 the Norwegians broke with Denmark, with which country they had been united since the sixteenth century. After a short struggle Norway was joined with Sweden in a kind of Home Rule. This was increasingly unpopular and the union was dissolved in 1905, when Prince Carl of Denmark was elected King by vote of the people.

railways and roads brought neighbours together who had formerly been seabound or mountain-ringed, these processes were in themselves disturbing, when they broke up a way of life virtually unchanged since the Middle Ages. The conflict between the older and the younger generation was more than a conflict between youth and age. It was the clash of two ways of life. During the seventeenth and eighteenth centuries, Norway had been largely undisturbed by the modification of European civilization, but now both political and economic repercussions were shaking her

The Norwegian, however, is not easy to shake. Dour, intelligent and highly argumentative, he holds fast to his own opinion as he holds to his few acres of land. His virtue is tenacity, his vice obstinacy. He is not interested in the arts, though given to strong views on law or theology ; local politics are his relaxation—there is yet today a high level both of intelligence and of passion in the conduct of local affairs. The small professional class and the merchant class, the leaders of local society, though they stand on their dignity are not cut off from the people. In a country where the majority are self-employed as farmers or sailors, the main characteristic is independence—a firm and sometimes fierce self-sufficiency that encourages sardonic freedom of speech. The Norwegian abroad, or among strangers, is strong and silent : at home he is more likely merely to be strong. The national character is a paradox in which the doggedness of Brand and the wild dreams of Peer are united.

In England the Norse strain prevails in parts of Yorkshire and the Lakes—and also in the Scottish Lowlands—but though a family likeness may be traced, there is a characteristic Norwegian temper which is not to be found out of Norway. The more famous stories of the Norwegian part in the war could not be told of other lands : the poems of Arnulf Øverland and Nordahl Grieg have a note of their own. They are low-pitched but weighted with power.[1]   The Norwegian

[1] Nordahl Grieg was one who felt that poetry should be lived through ; to share the experience of his generation, he insisted on flying with Bomber Command, and his plane was lost over Berlin on 2nd December, 1943.

may appear stolid and hard-headed, but in moments of excitement the stolidity disappears.   The strength of Norway is shown negatively, in endurance and control, in unshakable and ponderous consistency, qualities bred of life in a hard land ; but it is steel which strikes a spark out of flint ; and as an explosion is violent in proportion to the pressure released, sudden flashes of recklessness, blind to risk and deaf to good council, will leap out, instantaneous and shattering.[1]

Ibsen's plays are built on this national rhythm, the fundamental rhythm of the Norwegian character.   Each depends on a culmination of slow pressure and ends in an explosion.

It is not only in war that the rhythm alternates.   Hence proceeds the sober temper of daily life, with the national passion for dangerous sports, skiing, mountaineering, arctic exploration, the national devotion to the memories of Nansen and Amundsen.   Among Scandinavians, the wealthy Swedes and the stolid Danes look on the " mad Norsemen " with much the feeling of the Saxon toward the " mad Irish " or the " mad Highlander ", whilst the Norwegians, in their turn, reserve for their more numerous neighbours something of that pitying tolerance with which the Celt digests his instinctive superiority.

Alike in his obstinacy and his recklessness, Ibsen was true to his breed.   He knew what he wanted to be, and in spite of the personal timidity which made him pathetically grateful for recognition, he was not to be deflected either by direct attack or well-meant dissuasion.   " I will not follow good advice ! " he cried.   His absurd pride, his appalling outbursts

Arnulf Øverland was taken to a concentration camp in Poland by the Germans, but his songs passed all over Norway by word of mouth.   He has now returned safely to Oslo.

[1] On the one hand may be placed the story of the tanker's captain trying to entertain a passenger at dinner.   " Yes . . . when we sailed to Hong Kong we had a Chinese cook aboard." . . . Pause while the captain consumed two courses in silence.   " When he went ashore, he couldn't understand the other Chinese." . . . Pause while further quantities of food were consumed. . . . " He came from another part of China." . . . On the other hand, the story of the *Stord* running in under the guns of the *Scharnhorst* to fire her torpedoes, running in closer, as she boasted, than the three British destroyers who accompanied her, and drawing from the commander of the flotilla the startled comment " I thought *Stord* was going in to ram ! "

of temper when he fancied himself insulted were violent but shortlived. He exploded ; but again, on some occasions when an explosion might have been looked for, he was unexpectedly meek. He was taciturn and sour ; but he could be wonderfully patient with literary young ladies in search of good advice—especially if they were pretty and could turn a compliment neatly.

The national situation at this time called for the national qualities of tenacity and stubbornness, and invited occasional outbursts of justifiable national rage. Norway is built on the complementary ideas of personal independence and respect for law.[1] A Norwegian's home is decidedly his castle. Even in 1940 the Norwegians were not conscripted since there was no time to order mobilization, yet King Haakon rallied his whole people, and earned for himself the personal devotion which can be accorded only to a *chosen* leader. The natural fence of independence among people who are civilized is the Rule of Law. The Norwegians, with the Scots and the Dutch, probably have the highest conception of Law among the people of Western Europe. The State appears to the ordinary Norwegian less in its political or executive than in its judicial and legislative functions. This is natural in a land where the Executive has not become over-developed through the complexities of industrial or colonial administration, and where foreign policy can only be that of all small powers. The country is united on a basis of Law.[2] It was natural, indeed inevitable, that to Ibsen poetry should be thought of as a Doom-session on the soul.

Now Ibsen's Norway, though legally a separate kingdom, was not in her own eyes free. The King and the Executive could exercise a veto against decrees of the Storthing—one such

[1] This was written before the appearance of Sigmund Skard's analysis of Norwegian literature in *The Voice of Norway* (Hutchinson, 1944), which is based on the antithesis of freedom and law in the national tradition.

[2] Again, in 1940, the Norwegians would have been prepared to arrange a military capitulation, which would reflect no dishonour on a small people caught unawares ; but King Haakon rejected the political terms since these included illegal exercise of the royal prerogative in appointing a puppet Ministry. He refused to tamper with the legal basis of government.

crisis is behind the political references in *Rosmersholm*. Above
all, however, the Norwegian passion for independence chafed
against the position of junior partner in the double monarchy.

Ibsen's Norway, though becoming conscious of herself,
was still unwillingly united to Sweden and her feelings were,
in milder form, those of the Ireland of that date. The smallest
and poorest of the Scandinavian states, she was ruled politically
from Stockholm and culturally from Copenhagen. She had
not even a language of her own. A multiplicity of dialects
were spoken in the countryside ; the official language, Dano-
Norwegian, had only just come into use as a spoken tongue.
Ibsen was of the first generation who naturally wrote and
spoke in this form.[1] Already his writing sounds old-fashioned
in Norwegian ears, for since his day the progress of Norse
forms has ousted the Danish from the Riksmål, the official
language, whilst the strong development of the Landsmål, or
dialect speech, as a literary language, means that the vernacular
is now a second official language : both are taught in the
schools.

Ibsen, who was twenty years old in the year of revolutions,
1848, interested himself ardently in politics, though his
excursion into political journalism was commendably and
prudently brief. He had to build a literary and theatrical
tradition for Norway, to create and control his medium. To
him and his contemporaries, Vinje, Ivar Åsen and Bjørnson,
fell the kind of spadework which Spenser and the University
Wits did for England. The language had suddenly and
violently to be adapted to meet the changed needs which the

[1] " Quite early it is evident that Ibsen's language is freer, more flexible
than that of the Norwegian poets of the first half of the nineteenth century.
This is not only a result of his natural ease. . . . For the older Norwegian
writers the Danish language had been much more purely a book language
than it was for the new generation. . . . They did not think in that language, and therefore they wrote more heavily, less fluently than the Danes.
The generation born about 1830 had far less difficulty in this respect. At that
time, the Danish literary language had established itself in the circles of city
dwellers and people of the official or professional class as a natural spoken
language. It had adapted itself to certain characteristically Norwegian
accents in pronunciation, and it was felt to be genuinely a mother tongue."
(Koht, II, pp. 127-8.)

new conditions were imposing ; and as the new ideas of the
sixteenth century strained and disturbed the language of
England, then an outlying country on the fringe of European
culture, so the Norwegian language had to be adapted to the
new needs of the nineteenth century, and to much that had
gone before.

Ibsen was constantly experimenting in new forms and new
styles of verse, and all his early dramas were based on heroic
tales of old Norway, all pointed toward the national cause
which was more directly advocated in his polemical work.
His first play, *Cataline*, deals with a rebellion from the rebel's
point of view. *The Warrior's Barrow*, a romantic play of a
conventional kind, which he wrote almost at the same time,
contains a good deal of nationalist rhapsodizing on the part
of Blanka the Sicilian heroine, who dreams of the North, and
is duly carried off by a civilized and Christian Viking named
Gandolf. When he took over the Bergen theatre, Ibsen
found that there was simply no Norwegian drama to be
produced. The programmes consisted of Danish vaudeville
and French *Drame*. "Ibsen himself regarded it clearly as
his mission to write national drama. . . . He believed that
poetry should strengthen the power of achievement in a
people."[1] The immediate way was to reach back to Norway's glorious past, and to unite the old and new Norway
by establishing continuity. Hence national Romanticism in
Norway took the form of historic literature and writing on
historic themes together with revivals of the old Norse
speech-forms.

The Feast at Solhaug, Ibsen's first success, was written in the
ballad style, lavishly coloured with old Norse customs and
scenes : Ibsen had made a special study of the Norse ballads,
newly collected by Asbjørnson. *Lady Inger* was written
around the last great struggle for Norwegian independence ;
and though it was not strictly faithful to the letter of historic
events, its sentiments were so strongly anti-Danish that Ibsen
afterwards, in his sympathy for Denmark, toned them down.
The Warriors at Helgeland was modelled on the sagas, both in

[1] Koht, I, p. 88.

matter and in style.   True, he had read the sagas in a Danish translation and his attempt to reproduce the saga style now dates as curiously as Victorian Gothic architecture ; but prose was a novelty, and difficult for Ibsen, and he needed a model to work from.[1]

His next play *Kingmaking*—usually called *The Pretenders*— is the most nationalistic of all.   The conflict of Haakon and Skule is resolved in the triumph of the " great kingly thought " that there should be only one Norwav—the thought that Haakon conceives and Skule dies to preserve.   This play was Ibsen's second national success and has continued popular in Norway.[2]   The whole theme is the birth of nationalism, the birth of kingship, although in the final prophetic speech of Bishop Nicholas, Ibsen does not spare his country a severe warning.   Bishop Nicholas is an embodiment of the spirit of division and local rule which is the Norwegian's evil genius.

Kingmaking, with the exception of this speech, was written in prose, and no longer in the prose of the sagas, but in a good contemporary speech.   Soon after this, Ibsen suffered the Great Disappointment with Norway, and turned away from nationalism, and his hope of becoming a national poet.   He revised *Love's Comedy*, cutting out the ultra-Norwegian phrases ; and in *Peer Gynt* he satirized the national linguistic reforms.   At the Stockholm conference in 1869 he advocated a " Scandinavian orthography " and thenceforth practised it himself, in almost complete singularity.   And with *Peer Gynt* and the publication of his *Poems*, he gave up writing poetry.   He even spoke against poetry for the stage, alleging that it had done the art of acting much harm.[3]

The brilliant and lively phrases of his early plays have passed into the common speech of Norway.   They lose more

[1] ibid., II, p. 127.
[2] " The play is too closely related to the Norwegian national background. The great national challenge in it, the 'king's thought' is presented in a form that especially appeals to Norwegian national consciousness, and it is filled, one might perhaps say overburdened, with particular references to Norwegian history which may be clear enough to Norwegians but which make it seem somewhat remote to people of other nationalities." (ibid., I, p. 228.)
[3] ibid., II, p. 127.

obviously in translation than does the prose of the later plays. But it is doubtful if the loss is really more serious. For Ibsen's prose is dramatic, which means that in balance, movement and rhythm it is adapted for speaking ; and it is literature, which means that it is built upon the natural virtues of the tongue and upon Ibsen's personal idiom as he fashioned it to his needs. His writing can be understood only in terms of the Norse, with its clear, pungent but concrete vocabulary, its strong, live metaphors (" we felt our hearts *beat strongly towards him* ") [1] its lack of reverberation or overtones. It is as clear and fine as mountain air. Great play can be made by simple rhetorical devices, which stand out boldly, like a patterned weave thrown up on a plain cloth. In English, the cloth is dyed, shot with all the iridescent synonyms of a sophisticated and hybrid tongue, and Ibsen's effects are lost. His translators too were not concerned with the poetic use of language or with those sides of Ibsen's genius which were rooted in his race : his humour, which was exuberant and ironical,[2] his lyricism, his melancholy, and his piety. Swift, Burns and Emily Brontë shaken up together in a bag might produce something resembling Ibsen. The dehydrated Ibsen who is known through translations has little in common with any of the three.

It would be more than ungrateful to belittle the devoted work of William Archer, and his translations have the great merit of being literally honest. But they are in the translator's equivalent of Basic English, without form or comeliness. To take an example from the famous end of Act III of *Hedda Gabler*, Archer writes : " Now I am burning your child, Thea ! Burning it, curly-locks ! Your child and Eilert Løvborg's ! I am burning—I am burning your child ! " The original is : " Nu braender jeg dit barn, Thea ! Du med krushåret ! Dit og Eilert Løvborg's barn ! Nu braender—

---

[1] A description of the people's loyalty to King Haakon VII.
[2] At a party in a London flat the banter ran : " It is very difficult, all the servants are out today. . . . Please have some salmon, we caught it ourselves last Sunday. And the eggs, these are from our own hens. The hens belong to the flat, yes. Yes, today is the Crown Prince's birthday. He wanted so much to come to this party but I told him he couldn't. . . ."

nu braender jeg barnet ! " The heavy stresses, the tolling
vowels, the rasping consonants are the very life of the passage.
Archer built his version on the ugliest Cockney diphthong in
the English language. A flavour of the Northern dialects
which preserve so much of our Norse inheritance might best
convey the qualities of Ibsen's speech to an English reader.
" Every speech should be as fully flavoured as a nut or apple,
and such speeches cannot be written by anyone who works
among people who have shut their lips on poetry." [1]   Archer,
though he paid due reverence to Ibsen's powers in poetry,
was the author of The Old Drama and the New, and that
defence of Ibsen betrays the limits of his understanding of the
poet. It was not the poetry but the message that came first
with him. Nor was Archer's generation concerned with the
idiosyncrasies of national character ; Ibsen, in particular,
seemed a model citizen of the world. Later generations have
lost the optimistic hope that historic and geographic boundaries
are withering away to the final Marxist state : and if even in
terms of sociology such a loss has its compensations, in
literature it is pure gain. For literature is written with *living*
words ; Ibsen could not have written his plays in Basic
English, or in any tongue but Norse.

[1] Synge, preface to The Playboy of the Western World (1907).

Chapter Two

THE POET

Poems and early Works—" Love's Comedy "
" Brand "—" Peer Gynt "

THE greatness of Ibsen was shown only in exile. But the
world-famous artist was moulded and conditioned by the
young poet from whom he had so spectacularly cut himself
off. The greater the artist, the more inescapable are the
links between his various writings ; Ibsen himself stressed
that his works followed a pattern of their own and that their
order was significant.

The earliest plays and poems are experiments : *Cataline*,
Ibsen's *Titus Andronicus*, written in the apothecary's shop at
Grimstad, and published as a venture of faith at a friend's
expense—*The Warrior's Barrow, Olaf Liljekrans* and the three
historic plays which followed. These plays correspond in
Ibsen's career to that period when Shakespeare was shaping
his art in the chronicles and writing his " sugred sonets " as
relief. Ibsen, between his plays wrote poems that were
far from sugared, in which are reflected, in miniature, the
moods and even the themes of his latest work. Few critics
have defended the earliest plays of all, although the much-
derided *Olaf Liljekrans* has moments of fey poetry when the
mad mountain maid, Alfhild, the daughter of an even madder
skald, bursts into some rapturous chant. The play cannot
be accused of rambling, for there is no main subject from
which to digress. Silly, charming, utterly unpractical, as it
is, it is far preferable to the mélange of long-lost fathers,
poisoned goblets, coffins and secret strawberry-marks of *The
Warrior's Barrow, The Feast at Solhaug,* and *Lady Inger*. Ibsen's
two later historical plays, *The Warriors at Helgeland* and
Kingmaking are often praised for powerful characterization ;
Hjørdis, the Brynhild of the first play, is related to later
heroines, and Bishop Nicholas, Haakon and Skule, are rela-

tively complex figures, whilst the mere theme of *Kingmaking* makes it " the national saga play above all others ".[1] The cold fact remains, however, that all these plays are honest journey-work ; had they not been written by Ibsen they would certainly be unknown outside Norway. Ibsen did not become a great dramatist until he broke away from the stage. His dozen years' practical experience must have been useful, but he was not a successful manager, and he never became a man of the theatre in the same sense as Shakespeare or Molière.

The true power of Ibsen in these years is found in the handful of poems written in the 'fifties and early 'sixties, the best of which were collected into one volume in 1871. It is here that the Ibsen of the later work can be discerned. Brandes said that " in the battle of life a literary Pegasus was killed under Ibsen ", but it seems rather that the powers of the poet developed in Ibsen as a power to condense and focus and integrate, which later took prose drama as its vehicle.

Ibsen's *Digte* consists of about fifty poems, less than a third of his original output and many of them very much revised. Some are verse letters, others are political declamations on the Prussian-Danish war, the struggle for Norwegian independence, or the state of parties. The personal lyrics are selected from a much larger output. *In the Picture Gallery*, a sequence of twenty-five poems, remains as a title of only one lyric, though parts of the original, much revised, appear in the *Digte* under other names. Ibsen pared and reduced his poetry with a sternness he did not show to his early drama ; yet compared with anything he wrote later, these poems are passionate and unguarded. The invective is heady, the humour exuberant. There are several pieces of self-defence, a few rueful lyrics on the affair with Rikke Holst, the poem he wrote to his wife in thanks for her support against his difficulties. In all these we see the painful struggle of the sensitive and poverty-stricken young man against complacent established men, the chafing of the reformer against political restrictions, provincial inertia, the dead weight of life in a small, poor corner of the world.

[1] Koht, I, p. 227.

Ibsen's claim to be a poet rests however on the few symbolic lyrics in which he embodied his personal experience.[1] These poems are astonishing in their concentration and flexibility ; each is stamped with the impress of a keen personal experience. In these poems as nowhere else, Ibsen spoke out. Yet he spoke out, as a dramatist might be expected to do, in dramatic images. In each poem the feeling is embodied in a symbol—the tortured bear, the caged bird, the eiderduck, the miner, the petrel. It is not a static symbol, finely wrought, like those of Gautier, but a dramatic one ; in some of the poems a complete little drama is played out. There may or may not be a gloss, such as the last half of *Minds-Might* provides. First comes the terse account of the bear's dancing lesson, tied in a copper over a furnace whilst a barrel organ plays " Enjoy your life ! " to the poor brute. So whenever the bear hears that tune again, he dances, as if with pain, as he danced in the heated copper. Then the poet goes on

I too in the copper once found a seat. . . .[2]

and it is the recollection of this that makes him dance on the " feet " of the verse. Here the intolerable quickness of sensibility that the symbol exposes is controlled by the sardonic tone of the poem, and the savage rhythm of the long couplets, which seem to echo the drone of the barrel organ. The use of the tortured bear reduces the initial experience almost to pure sensation, but the tone and rhythm modify this original simplicity.

This is the method which on a much larger scale Ibsen used in *The Wild Duck*, a play which is particularly connected with another early poem, *The Eider-Duck*. The eider-duck, building its nest on the fjord, is robbed of its nest-feathers by the fisherman—once, twice and again. In the original version it ultimately dies, but in the final version it spreads its wings :

[1] e.g. *With a Water Lily, Minds-Might, Bird and Bird Catcher, The Petrel, Absent, Fear of Light, The Miner, The Eider-Duck, Burnt Ships, Stars in Nebulæ,* and the sequence *On the Vidda*.

[2] *Jeg selv sad engang i kedlen nede.* . . .

To the South, to the South, to the coasts of the Sun ! . . .[1]

The intensely personal bitterness behind the description is a most direct and poignant comment on Ibsen's early struggle ; but in many of these lyrics the symbol of the tortured animal reoccurs.[2] Even the lighter poems are for the most part melancholy in tone. *With a Water Lily* has a beautiful lilting rhythm which suggests the water lily rocking on the surface of the deadly stream, which to Ibsen symbolizes the beauty and the deadliness of love ; yet there is a half-surrender to the danger, a caressive relaxing in the repetitions.[3]

Burnt Ships is Ibsen's only word on the pangs of exile. In the gigantic shadowy bridge of the steamer's smoke, uniting Norway and Italy, and still more in the figure of the horseman who every night sweeps north to the " Snowland " there is vague nightmare horror, trodden under by the stern beat of the rhythm. Ibsen himself trod his homesickness down ; here for this once his control has not suppressed the ineradicable need. The poem was not written till 1871, when Ibsen had been in exile for seven years ; but his feelings had not softened with time.

A number of these poems deal with the artist's experience in creation. " I was an artist first and foremost," says Rubek in the latest play, and in these early poems the act of creation is seen as a day dream (*Building Plans*), an escape from the intolerable pressure of the world (*The Fear of Light*), an obscure toil (*The Miner*) and a judgment of oneself (*A Poem*). In *The Miner*, a very early poem but much revised, the poet is above all uncertain of himself. He does not know the answer of his life's endless riddle, and the spirits of the mine do not reveal it to him. Still, he must down : that is the way to peace for him ; so he hacks his way on in darkness.

---

[1] *Mod syd, mod syd til en solskins-kyst ! . . .*
[2] e.g. *Bird and Bird Catcher, The Petrel, Complications.*
[3] This poem was addressed to Marie Thoresen, the poet's young sister-in-law : she died a few years later. Ibsen loved and mourned her. Her figure may be the inspiration for Asta, in *Little Eyolf,* whose last gift to Alfred is a handful of water lilies from the tarn.

Nay, in the depths, down must I bore.
There is peace for evermore.
Burst my way then, iron hammer,
To the heart's deep-hidden chamber!

Blow on hammer—blow I shower
To my lifetime's final hour.
Without a single streak of morning,
Without the achievement of the dawning.[1]

The superb use of weight in these lines will be obvious even to those who have little Norwegian. But it is no mere onomatopœic feat.[2] Energy darkened with gloom is the substance of the poem, and the miner is not only the most dramatic but the most inwardly particular figure in all the lyrics.

A poem which belongs to this group though it was not written till 1886, and is solitary in that decade, is the astonishing *Stars in Nebulæ*. The comparison with Keats's *On first looking into Chapman's Homer* is obvious but Ibsen is describing the creative, not the inspirational process, the gradual drawing together of the "light-mist coiling and shrunk to a star". The splendour of the poem, brilliant with light and tense with muscular imagery of circling and shrinking forces, lies in its coiling flexible rhythm. It is written in the metre of *In Memoriam* and the internal rhymes reinforce the dominant feeling of concentric coils. No happier image of Ibsen's peculiar power as a writer could have been found. Techni-

---

[1] *Nej, i dybet må jeg ned;*
der er fred fra evighed.
Bryd mig vejen, tunge hammer,
til det dulgtes hjerte-kammer!

Hammerslag på hammerslag
Indtil livets sidste dag.
Ingen morgenstråle skinner :
Ingen håbets sol oprinder.

[2] Incidentally it did not appear in the first version. The fact that Ibsen's poems date from his very earliest years as a writer and yet are related to his very latest dramas is a striking example of the homogeneity of his work. This poem was first drafted in 1851, yet it has an obvious relationship to *John Gabriel Borkman* (written 1895–6).

cally the poem is probably his greatest achievement in lyric ;
the vision at once grand and void of detail, free from any
association except the awe of " the starry heavens above and
the moral law within " is the perfect equivalent of the artist
in contemplation of his work. This embodies the deepest
experience of Ibsen's life : he too after all was first and foremost an artist.[1]

Only in this poem is the creative process described as other
than painful : the poet had been cruelly tormented by Pan
for the fashioning of his reed pipe. This was a theme on
which Kierkegaard had written bitterly in *Either-Or*, in words
which seem to be echoed in the bitter poem Ibsen wrote for
the millenary celebrations of 1872, in which he thanked
Norway for the gift of sorrow.

> What is a poet ? An unhappy man who conceals deep tor-
> ments in his heart but whose lips are so formed that when a
> groan or a shriek streams out, then it sounds like beautiful music.
> His fate is like that of those unfortunates who in Philaris' ox
> were slowly tortured by a slow fire, whose shriek could not reach
> the tyrant's ear to affright him ; it sounded to him like sweet
> music. . . . I tell you I had rather be a swineherd upon the
> flats of Amigar and be understood of the swine than be a poet
> and be misunderstood of men.[2]

The theme of that work, the necessity for choice, the
" conflict between the æsthetic and the ethical ", as Kierkegaard
termed it, was the groundwork of much of Ibsen's early
work. In particular it was the groundwork of *On the Vidda*,[3]
a long poem in nine sections, written in a variety of metres,
which seems to contain much of the material for *Love's
Comedy* and *Brand*. This poem was written in 1859-60, two

[1] He once described how he gradually came to see his characters more and
more clearly : at first he knew them as one might know fellow-passengers
in a train : in the second draft, as one might know acquaintances at a spa :
but by the third draft he knew them through and through.

[2] *Either-Or* : first Diapsalmata. When this was written Swinson and
Lowrie's translation (Oxford, 1945) was not available. The reference there
is Vol. I, p. 15.

[3] *Vidda* is really untranslatable : it is the desolate upland waste, heather,
rock and scree, of the wilder parts of Norway.

years before the final appearance of *Love's Comedy*—which however had been begun in 1858—and six years before *Brand*. *Love's Comedy* and the poem were both begun within a year of Ibsen's marriage, and in both the subject is the artist's duty to renounce love, marriage and all ordinary ties for a life on the mountain peaks. The significance of this poem for an understanding of Ibsen's work justifies a résumé of its story.

On the Vidda opens with a wooing, on the hill side, in the summer night. The girl pleads, the trolls laugh, the lover wins.

> *I saw her sweetness and her fear,*
> *Felt her young body shake.*[1]

The morning sees him off to the hills for reindeer. He sees his mother down on the bleaching-square far below as he goes, bidding the girl prepare for the bridal.

Then up in the heather, he lies thinking of her and of his love, even wishing that her path may be difficult so that he can smooth it, and challenge God Himself in protection of her.

Suddenly a stranger appears, a hunter from the south, with cold eyes like mountain lakes. A strange fear seizes the lover, yet instinctively he knows there is a tie between the hunter and himself. The hunter calls him up to the mountain heights, to action instead of to dreams.

So he stays in the mountains all summer and by autumn he loathes the valley. He plans to bring his mother and his bride up to the mountains to live in the spring. An impulse to see them comes too late, for by now all the paths are snow-bound. He knows that he can no longer share the life of the valley.

The next section is in winter starlight. The lover is acclimatized to solitude, yet hearing the Christmas bells, he has a second spasm of longing ; the Strange Hunter appears and catches the thought as it leaves him. At that moment a glow appears from his mother's cot : it is afire. The hunter coolly

---

[1] *Jeg så kun hun var raed og fin,*
og kendte hvor hun skalv.

points out the beauty of the fire and advises on the best way
to get the view. Then he disappears and leaves the son
with his blood freezing and burning, yet acknowledging
after all, in spite of himself, the beauty of the scene.

In the last section, it is summer. The lover lies in the
warm ling whilst down below he sees a bridal procession
winding through the trees—his bride with another man.
And with that final blow he discovers that he has grieved
his heart free at last. *Cantat vacuus.* He curves his hand to
get the perspective right. He can accept his own broken
life as material for contemplation ; self-steeled he looks on
at joy from above life's snow-line. The Strange Hunter
reappears and tells him he is now free, and the lover acknowledges that although his heart is petrified, his life is broken,
he can now endure life on the heights.

> *Now I am steel-set : I follow the call*
> *To the height's clear radiance and glow.*
> *My lowland life is lived out : and high*
> *On the* vidda *are God and Liberty—*
> *Whilst wretches live fumbling below.*[1]

In a letter written in 1870 Ibsen described his intellectual
development at this time :

The Warriors at Helgeland I wrote while I was engaged to be
married. For Hjørdis I used the same model that I took afterwards for Svanhild in Love's Comedy. Not until I was married,
did more serious interests take possession of my life. The first
outcome of this was a long poem, On the Vidda. The desire for
emancipation which pervades that poem did not however receive
its full expression till I wrote Love's Comedy, a book which gave
rise to much talk in Norway. People mixed up my personal
affairs in the discussion and I fell greatly in public estimation.
The only person at that time who approved of the book was my

---

[1] *Nu er jeg stålsat : jeg følger der bud*
Der byder i højden at vandre !
Mit lavlandsliv han jeg levet ud ;
heroppe på vidden er frihed og Gud
dernede famler de andre.

wife. Hers is exactly the character desiderated by a man of mind—she is illogical, but has a strong poetic instinct, a broad and liberal mind and an almost violent antipathy to all petty considerations. All this my countrymen did not understand, and I did not choose to make them my father-confessors. So they excommunicated me. All were against me.[1]

This passage lends only rather dubious support to the general belief that Susannah was the model for Hjørdis and Svanhild. That a personal renunciation of an agonizing kind is embodied here it would be futile to deny. Ibsen was later accused of æstheticism; of choosing to be an artist rather than a man. But this is not æstheticism in Kierkegaard's sense—eudæmonism, the pursuit of happiness. It involves a hard act of choice. What the Strange Hunter offers on the heights is action at its most strenuous—thought which has the force of deeds and "strengthens the power of achievement in a people", and which is depicted in the mountain visions of the latest plays, and in the poem *On the High Fjell*. The keenness and delicacy of mountain air, the hunter's life of isolation are the very opposite of æstheticism, involving that same renunciation of the sensuous which is symbolized also, later, as the murder of the child. On the purely literal plane, however, the allegory is a little lacking in co-ordination and what the lover actually achieves on the heights, beyond the process of steeling himself, cannot be put into concrete terms. A quality of life is indicated, the quality which enables him to see his choice, make it and hold to it. Life in the valley with his love calls to the eudæmonist in him—who is defeated.

For Kierkegaard too, the act of deciding that a choice must be made between the æsthetical and the ethical is itself the first and most important choice.

What then is it that I distinguish in my Either-Or? is it good and evil? No, I would merely bring you to the point where this choice has significance for you. On that everything depends. If only a man can be brought to stand at the cross-

---

[1] *Corr.*, pp. 198–9.

roads where there is no escape for him, but to choose, he will choose aright. My Either-Or does not first of all designate the choice between good and evil : it designates the choice of choosing between good and evil, or excluding such an alternative.[1]

Ibsen had been brought to choose. The fates had brought their man to the greatest obstacle he could confront without despair. And it was the act of choice which made the artist. As Yeats said of Dante and Villon, he could now turn all to mask and image, because he had suffered and had chosen to suffer.

Such masters—Dante and Villon let us say—would not, when they speak through their art, change their luck : yet they are mirrored in all the suffering of desire. The two halves of their nature are so completely joined that they seem to labour for their objects, and yet to desire whatever happens, being at the same instant predestinate and free, creation's very self.[2]

It may be that Ibsen had not yet clearly seen what his choice involved. But in the " desire for emancipation ", with all its suggestion of Victorian rationalism, he recorded not an impulse towards a new creed, but towards a way of living—the way of the artist. It was to become increasingly clear to him what were the limits and what the price of the life he had chosen.

2

Having written this stark poem, Ibsen went on to write his wittiest and sprightliest comedy, as a variation on the same theme. In the play there are a sufficient number of verbal reminiscences to prove that, in spite of his disclaimers,

[1] Kierkegaard, *Either-Or*, ed. cit., II, p. 142. This passage seems to have suggested the cross-roads scene in *Peer Gynt*.
[2] See ch. I, p. 12 above. Yeats, loc. cit., p. 338.

Love's Comedy and *Brand* are deeply indebted to Kierkegaard.[1]
The story of *Love's Comedy* is indeed akin to the love story
of Kierkegaard and Regina Olsen, which, however, Ibsen
could scarcely have known. Kierkegaard renounced the
woman he loved, and who loved him in turn, though much
of his work was written for and around Regina. He renounced her because he was a man "under penance" and
by temperament and calling he felt bound not to marry. It
was from Kierkegaard that Ibsen learnt to formulate the
problem of *On the Vidda*, and learnt to probe and dissect
his own motives and his own heart.[2] *Love's Comedy*, begun
soon after his marriage but not brought out until six years
later, contains several strata of thought, overlaid and not
always related ; but the main theme is substantially that of
the choice of *On the Vidda*. It is the first dramatic work
to be stamped with the mark of Ibsen.

The poet found himself in a very obvious way. Falk, the
hero, speaks for Ibsen throughout ; he had not put himself
quite so indubitably in the centre of the picture before. Falk,
the young poet, iconoclastic breaker-up of tea-parties, flutters
the dove-cotes, outrages the conventions and finally stalks off
to the mountains on his life work, leaving his Svanhild to
the sober protection of the wise old merchant Guldstad.
Because Svanhild and Falk love so passionately, they cannot
bear that their love should decay into habit and acquire the
virtues of contractual fidelity. Svanhild first sees the truth
and cries ardently :

> *We are born of Spring*
> *And never to us shall the Autumn come,*

[1] Ibsen read Kierkegaard at Grimstad through the kindness of Miss Crawfurd
(Koht, I, p. 33). "On the whole there was almost certainly no one in his
own times to whom Ibsen was as much indebted as Kierkegaard" (ibid.,
p. 63). Pastor Lammers, a disciple of Kierkegaard, was one of the models for
Brand, as Ibsen confirmed to Hedvig : "The town passed thro' a period of
spiritual storms, which spread from there over a wide area. I have always
loved stormy weather. And though absent I went thro' this tempestuous
period with you. To this a part of my literary production bears witness"
(*Corr.*, pp. 438–9).
[2] Koht, I, p. 169.

The singing bird grow silent in thy breast
And nest no longer when the trees are bare. . . .
Our love that, radiant, triumphs now so sure
Shall sickness shrivel or old age weaken down ?—
Die, rather, as it lived, youthful and strong ! [1]

This would seem a theme for tragedy rather than comedy.[2]
To save their love they must forfeit their happiness, because
they have touched the topmost peak and henceforth love
must decline.

If 'twere now to die,
'Twere now to be most happy. . . .

and so unless they part, at the Day of Judgment they will
have to confess that they lost their treasure in the wastes of
daily living. Svanhild throws Falk's ring into the fjord :

Till the world's end, within the ocean
Lie low, my dream—an offered sacrifice.
Now I have lost thee for a lifetime long,
But won thee in Eternity's sunrise.[3]

So madly heroic a gesture is but the inevitable sequel to the
satiric exposure of domesticity by Falk. In vain do Pastor

[1] *Vi er Børn af Våren*
bag den skal ikke komme nogen Høst,
da Sanger fuglen tier i dit Bryst
og aldrig laenges did, hvor den er båren. . . .
vor Kaerlighed, den glade, sejerskaekke
skal Sot ej taerre på, ej Ælde svaekke—
dø skal den, som den leved, ung og rig !

[2] The English reader will think at once of Shelley's *When the Lamp is
Shattered*—written in a metre curiously akin to Ibsen's ; and of Deirdre's
farewell to Alban in Synge's play : " It's this hour we're between the day-
time and a night when there is sleep for ever, and isn't it a better thing
to be following on to a near death, than to be bending the head down, and
dragging with the feet, and seeing one day a blight showing on love where
it is sweet and tender ? . . . It is not a small thing to be rid of grey hairs
and the loosening of the teeth. It was the choice of life we had in the clear
woods and in the grave we're safe surely. . . ."

[3] *Til verdens Fald, immellem Havets Siv*
Duk ned, min Drøm—dig offrer jeg isteden.
Nu har jeg mistet dig for dette Liv—
Men jeg har vundet dig for Evigheden.

Stråmand, father of twelve children, and Styver, the civil
servant who is saving up to get married, urge that

> To build a happy fireside clime,
> For weans and wife,
> That's the true pathos and sublime
> Of human life.

Falk replies that these admirable feelings are not *love*. " I
will not hall-mark brass as gold ! " and when Guldstad applies
the *argumentem ad hominem* to Falk's own love for Svanhild,
not only do the lovers part, but Svanhild accepts the logical
conclusion and bestows herself on her solid and paternal
admirer—she whom Falk had singled out as so different from
the tattlers at her mother's tea table, and to whom he had
pleaded:

> If die you must, then live beforehand,
> Be mine in the springtime of God's earth :
> Soon in the gilded cage you'll stand,
> The woman die, the lady come to birth. . . .[1]

Svanhild at first rejects him because he is too much the poet
and insufficiently the man of action, and he wants her only
as a reed to play on :

> Paper poems in the desk can stay :
> To live, your poetry must be lived through.
> Thus only can you reach the Mountain Way.
> Now make your choice : it lies between the two.[2]

Only when Falk has finally disrupted the party with his
sermon on Love and Tea, his outrageous suggestion that the
best love is illicit love, does Svanhild throw herself into his
arms.

[1] *Men skal De åndigt dø, da lev forinden !*
Vaer min i Herrens vårlige Natur
De kommes tidsnok, i det gyldne Bur
Der trives Damen, men der sygner kvinden. . . .
[2] *Papirets Digtning hører Pulten til,*
og kun den levende er livets eje
kun den har faerdselret på Højdens Veje :
men vaelg nu mellen begge den De vil.

The final fate of Svanhild is in fact that which she had rejected for herself in Act I : she resigns him in order to be Falk's inspiration, the matter of his song. Falk is filled with a divine afflatus of destruction, which extends from the wrecking of his sitting-room—where he breaks up the furniture as a symbol of his new life[1]—to the final song which he sings on his way to the heights with the rest of " Young Norway's Choir ".

> *And what if I run my ship aground—*
> *Oh, still it was splendid to sail !* [2]

The play is Falk's ; and in such a spate of revolutionary ardour there is no chance for the " he and she ". Svanhild and Falk fire each other, but neither of them is drawn as a person in love with another person. *Love's Comedy* is not a play of character at all—which is why it is not a tragedy— but a play of ideas and of caricature. The different rôles are sharply distinguished, especially among the minor characters —wicked caricatures of respectable love in its various stages. Falk and Svanhild are vehicles for the author's ideas, an arrangement which makes Falk at least intelligible, but leaves Svanhild with a contradictory rôle. The verse is highly patterned, the cut-and-thrust runs at top speed but the two strains—mocking comedy and heroic ardour—do not always blend smoothly. The neatly contrived misunderstandings, which here and there give a semblance of plot, are too unimportant to jar—they are unnoticed : but Falk's discourse on Love and Tea shows particularly well the difficulties of combining revolutionary idealism and satiric iconoclasm. It is as if Shelley had tried to write *Epipsychidion* and *Swellfoot the Tyrant* at the same time.

Never again did Ibsen write so wittily, or, except in *Peer Gynt*, so exuberantly. The play is in many ways immature, but its headlong and happy vitality carries the reader along. It is Ibsen's *Love's Labour's Lost*, and though, as in that play,

---

[1] The reformer in *The Wild Duck* also wrecks his room in a zeal for reform ! Is there perhaps some personal memory behind these two domestic upheavals ?
[2] *Og har jeg end sejlet min Skude på Grund,*
O, så var det dog dejligt at fare ! Cf. p. 58.

"Jack has not Jill ", Falk, like Berowne, has his own reward in his unquenchable and dazzling *livsglaede* [1]. The delicate beauty of the Northern spring breathes through the description a tonic air into the very setting, which is a garden by the fjord. Although Ibsen was thirty-four when he finished it, the play reads like the work of a much younger man. It was his first play about contemporary life, and may in a sense be called his first true drama, the first in which he found a theme, a style and an accent which were completely his own.

The scandal was all he could have hoped for. In Act III Falk had seen himself like the Children of Israel setting out from Egypt to the promised land : he knew the way lay through the desert of contempt. In this play Ibsen finds what was to be his great motive power : the joy of righteous anger, of exposure and dissection of the Lie.

> *I go to Freedom through Disdain's parched sand.*
> *For me a path shall open in the waves.*
> *The hostile hordes, foul armies of the Lie,*
> *Shall find there, deep and dark, their destined graves !* [2]

A little light satire on the continental betrothal ceremony, the twittering and pryings of innumerable maiden aunts, might not have come amiss. But an attack on the institution of marriage itself, and on the clerical weakness for a well-endowed " call " was not at all well received—especially from the newly-married son-in-law of the late Dean Thoresen of Christ Church ! Ibsen found himself fiercely and crushingly denounced. The play could not be staged, for no one would put it on ; and the Church Department took its revenge for Ibsen's attack on the fruits of Establishment by intervening to quash his appeal for a Poet's Stipend on the Civil List.

After this, Ibsen passed through the most desperate period

[1] A quite untranslatable word usually rendered " the joy of life ".
[2] *Jeg går til Frihed gennem Døgnets Ørk,*
for mig er Fremkomst selv i Havets Fjaere :
men Fiendens Fylking, Løgnens fule Laere,
Skal finde der sin Gravtomt, dyb og mørk !

of his life. He was ill, destitute and without prospects. *Kingmaking* was a success but he was overwhelmed by the Great Disappointment of Norway's neutrality in the Prussian-Danish War ; and his next play was written in exile.

To Edmund Gosse he said :

Love's Comedy should be really regarded as a forerunner of *Brand*, for in it I have represented the contrast in our present state of society between the actual and the ideal in all that relates to love and marriage.[1]

To Bjørnson on the other hand he stressed rather the difference between the works written before and after his exile :

If I were asked to tell at this moment what has been the chief result of my stay abroad, I should say that it consisted in my having driven out of myself the æstheticism which had a great power over me—an isolated æstheticism with a claim to independent existence. Æstheticism of this kind seems to me now as great a curse to poetry as theology is to religion. You have never been troubled with it. You have never gone about looking at things through your hollowed hand [like the hero of *On the Vidda*].

Is it not an inexpressibly great gift of fortune to be able to write ? But it brings with it great responsibility : and I am now sufficiently serious to realize that and to be very severe with myself. An æsthete in Copenhagen once said to me " Christ is really the most interesting phenomenon in the world's history ". The æsthete enjoyed him as the glutton does the sight of an oyster. I have always been too strong to become a creature of that type : but what the intellectual asses might have made of me if they had had me all to themselves, I know not : it was you, dear Bjørnson, who prevented them doing as they would with me ![2]

[1] *Corr.*, p. 237.
[2] ibid., pp. 86-7. This passage was written in 1865, the letter to Gosse seven years later in 1872. But Ibsen's pronouncements on his own works seem often to be coloured by a temporary mood. He was most averse from giving any explanations or comments : he would hardly ever admit indebtedness to any other writer : he would always be polite to anyone who spoke favourably of his work, and extremely sharp with anyone who ventured upon criticism !

Alas ! it was Bjørnson who said in later years, after they had quarrelled : "Ibsen is not a man, he's a pen ! " In *Love's Comedy* can be discerned some of the grounds of the hard choice that gave opportunity for such a judgment. Falk did not sacrifice his love to poetry : he sacrificed, as Ibsen would say, the actuality of love to the ideal. In the first exalted moment of such a sacrifice the presence of the actual remains as a species of mirage, exciting and stimulating, so that the poet feels he has achieved the best of both worlds. But as the mirage fades, the implications of the choice are revealed.

3

The appearance of *Brand*, in 1866, established Ibsen in Scandinavia. He won both fame and independence ; the Storthing granted his pension and a travelling stipend, thanks to the convenient illness of the ecclesiastic who had previously opposed it. But of far greater importance than outward success was the fact that Ibsen had found himself. It was himself that he put into *Brand*, his struggle, his choice, his disappointment.

> It came into being as the result of something which I had not observed but experienced ; it was a necessity for me to free myself from something which my inner man had done with, by giving poetic form to it ; and when by this means I had got rid of it, my book had no longer any interest for me. . . . One must have something to create from, some life-experience. The author who has not that, does not create : he only writes books.[1]

Brand sums up Ibsen's inner story to that moment, and in writing it he exorcized his own past. Not for many years was he again to be autobiographical in the drama. The conflict was resolved ; or in Ibsen's own words, the poison was ejected.[2] His own desperate choice to stick to his calling,

---

[1] *Corr*, p. 193.
[2] " During those days [i.e. the Prussian triumph over Denmark] *Brand* began to grow within me like an embryo. When I arrived in Italy, the work

if need be to sacrifice wife and child—an anxiety which is also reflected indirectly in the poem *Terje Vigen*—he could only justify by thinking of himself as involved in a war and his family as war's victims. The Great Disappointment had destroyed his hopes; he could no longer centre his life on work for a free Norway, as he had done in *Kingmaking*. What horrified Ibsen was her infirmity of purpose, the fact that Norway had shuffled out of what he thought was her moral obligation into non-intervention and appeasement, and was complacently unconscious of her guilt. Substitute for Denmark, Spain or Czecho-Slovakia; for Norway, England; and for 1864, 1938; the position becomes painfully clear.

The personal choice which was attested in *On the Vidda* and *Love's Comedy*—to be a poet first and foremost—was deepened and intensified by this intervening experience. Not only must the poet stand alone : he must be prepared to fight both within and without : " Here stand I : I can no other." Such was " the demand of the ideal ".

Although Ibsen disclaimed any debt to Kierkegaard— whilst admitting that he had drawn upon the story of Kierkegaard's disciple Lammers, who had converted his own family in his native town of Skien—it was the general opinion that Ibsen had put a good deal of Kierkegaard into *Brand*. Kierkegaard too demanded that a man should give his All. For Kierkegaard too the strength of the will to choose was the first necessity of salvation. He first put before his generation the need for absolute self-surrender to the will of God—a drastic, complete and unqualified submission to the Other, which could only be made by a will in itself trained and

of unification there had already been completed by a spirit of sacrifice that knew no bounds. . . . It is a great mistake to suppose that I have depicted the life and career of Kierkegaard (I have read very little of Kierkegaard and understood even less). That Brand is a clergyman is really immaterial : the demand is made in all walks of life—in love, in art, etc. Brand is myself in my best moments. . . . During the time I was writing *Brand* I had on my desk a glass with a scorpion in it. From time to time the little animal was ill. Then I used to give it a piece of soft fruit, upon which it fell furiously and emptied into it its poison—after which it was well again. Does not something of the same kind happen with us poets ? " (ibid., pp. 199–200.)

powerful. The lack of such a will might make religion itself an offence.

> Let others complain that our times are corrupt : I complain that they are contemptible for they are without passion. People's thoughts are thin and miserable like lace girls, the impulses of their hearts too weak to be sinful.[1]

For Kierkegaard the integration of the whole man was the reward of the choice to submit. " You stand to gain what is the principal thing in life—to gain yourself, to inherit yourself." [2]

Kierkegaard's *Journals* are probably the most unrelenting and complex work of self-dissection ever written. His morbid self-consciousness led him to adopt all sorts of disguises, pseudonyms, and wheels within wheels, but he knew that he was a man singled out for a special dispensation, and that his rôle was to suffer and to write for posterity. In the variety and penetration of his psychological analysis he stands closer to the later works of Ibsen than to these early plays but by the cirsumstances of his life Kierkegaard was absorbed in the problem which figures so largely in *Brand*—the sins of the fathers visited on the children. His own father, who laboured under a terrible conviction of sin, brought Kierkegaard up in the stern creed that he was set apart and marked out for wrath. A lonely and unnatural childhood prepared him for a life almost more devoid of event than Ibsen's, and dominated as exclusively by the sense of a calling. In *Brand* Ibsen has embodied such a hereditary curse in the figures of the murderer's children and of Gerd ; the career of Brand himself begins in expiation of his mother's sin.

But the strongest link between the two writers is their attack on institutional religion. Kierkegaard's attack on the blindness and worldliness of the Church was of a satiric and mordant bitterness which must have appealed to Ibsen.

[1] Quoted by Koht, I, p. 272. His pages on the indebtedness of *Brand* to Kierkegaard (pp. 272–7) are the best balanced account of the matter. (The context is *Either-Or*, ed. cit., Vol. I, p. 22.)

[2] Quoted Lowrie, *Søren Kierkegaard* (Oxford University Press, 1939), p. 83. *Either-Or*, ed. cit., Vol. II, p. 138.

Kierkegaard himself felt entirely cut off from the Church of his day, and ended in a wilderness as solitary as the Ice Kirk. The disciples of Kierkegaard in Skien, the party which Ibsen's family joined, separated themselves from the State Church, and Hedvig's husband was threatened with the loss of his livelihood as a result.

The student of religion will probably feel that *Brand* is an " example of illegitimate interpretation of Søren Kierkegaard, who might have demanded ' All or Nothing ' but who would not have sanctioned such a ' teleological suspension of the ethical ' as the sacrifice of the child ".[1] It may be thought, however, that the self-torture of Kierkegaard was even more pitiful than that of Brand, who sacrificed the life of his child only because he felt that, like Abraham, he was specially called to do so, and that his parishioners' souls were being weighed against his son's body. Brand was a martyr and a tyrant : Kierkegaard too was something of a martyr and to himself the most ingenious and most implacable of tyrants.[2]

This play, produced at the very nadir of his fortunes and his hopes, took its final shape quite suddenly in Ibsen's mind. In its first draft he wrote it as an epic ; but after nearly two years' work, one day in St. Peter's he suddenly had an inspiration of how the whole thing should be. Without more ado he threw over all that he had done and started again. He wrote with great rapidity, and finished the play in its present form in less than six months.

Brand (the name means both *fire* and *sword*) stands at the beginning of Ibsen's work as *When we Dead Wake* at the end—a poetic statement cast in dramatic form, but not in the strict

[1] ibid., pp. 10–11. Kierkegaard himself however had been sacrificed by his father and the spiritual bleakness which Michael Kierkegaard forced upon his little son was perhaps worse than exposure to the physical rigour of winter.

[2] He made extraordinary attempts to blacken himself in the eyes of Regina, to spare her pain over the broken engagement. He regularly showed himself at theatres and parties for a few moments to give an impression of heartless gaiety. And when, after two years of this masquerading—including an unwelcome visit abroad which he undertook only for this end—Regina one day nodded to him at Church the effect was overwhelming. He wrote pages about it ; the nod was a major event in his life. It was the last episode of his love affair.

sense a play. It was considered by the Germans to be influenced by *Faust* but they have in common only the general features of the romantic poetic drama, where the hero debates the problem of his own salvation in conspicuous independence of lesser things—whether that hero be Faustus, Prometheus or Cain. *Brand* is inevitably the Norwegian version of the great European drama. Shut in his northern fjord, Brand's first self-conquest is to subdue himself to working in obscurity, not to go out and convert the world. He sacrifices his mother because he will not compromise with her miserly habits. She must renounce all before he will admit her to the sacrament. He sacrifices his child because he will not desert his flock. He sacrifices his wife because he forbids her to mourn and purges her of natural longing at the cost of her physical existence.

He sacrifices his ambition of building a new church because the people would remain satisfied with the external fabric. He tries to lead the people towards his vision, which is not of this world ; here too he fails, and finds himself alone in the Trolls' Church, the Ice Kirk, where he is tempted by a Spectre in the form of his dead wife, suggesting to him that he unwill all he has done. At the last moment, Brand receives illumination, and a vision of " life's summer-kingdoms ", though with Gerd the troll-girl, he is buried in the avalanche as a Voice proclaims " *Deus Caritatis* ".

Brand had always been tormented by the struggle between his Will and his Nature, which rising as the Spectre of his lost love openly woos him to renounce perfection of the will, while airy voices remind him that he is but flesh, and perfection is not for him. He rejects the tempters ; but when Gerd sees in him the stigmata of the crucifixion and hails him as a saviour, this final blasphemy reveals to Brand the Trolls' Church which in hideous parody had always overshadowed his own.[1] At last, he renounces Pride, calling on the name of the Crucified God Who is Love but Whom he had never known. The ice of his nature melts ; but the

[1] Gerd drives home the point to Brand : " A churchgoer after all ! "
See below, p. 52.

ruin of the Trolls' Church in which he stands involves his
own death.

A final Pisgah-sight of love cannot reverse the whole play.
Brand's struggle has been solely to purify the Will, to make
himself a blank tablet for God's writing. His view has
dominated without any implied reservations or undertones :
Brand *is* the play. Moreover the answer to his last question
is in its circumstance dreadful and mysterious—not the Voice
of the Crucified but that of Jahweh from Sinai, delivering a
stark enunciation.[1] Brand's will had been set towards God,
but his love towards the humanity which he renounced ;
there he had loved truly, and every step was torment to him,
but in Whose name and Whose spirit was the renunciation
made ?

> *Who then devised the torment ?   Love.*
> *Love is the unfamiliar Name*
> *Behind the hands that wove*
> *The intolerable shirt of flame*
> *Which human power cannot remove. . . .*[2]

Such doctrine is only tolerable to those whom the miseries
of the world would else involve in the Manichean heresy.
Such was Ibsen himself, and such he made Brand.

Brand's theology is summed up in his motto *All or Nothing* [3]
(" *Intet—eller Alt* "). He is in revolt against compromise,
against what has been called Christianity-and-water. His
God is not the traditionally decrepit God the Father, but is
" young, like Hercules "—or the Christ of *A Dream of the
Rood.*

> *Upon God's love alone I call—*
> *It is not mild and flexible,*

[1] Nothing is here of the positive, defining, enriching qualities of a felt
experience : nothing of the vision implicit in Jahweh's speech from the
whirlwind to Job, or the greater vision of St. Paul's hymn to love. Brand
sees only that his own vision of God has been incomplete : but it is this incomplete vision which has been presented throughout the play as it stands.

[2] T. S. Eliot, *Four Quartets* (Faber, 1945), p. 12.

[3] The Bishop of Oslo has recently described how important a part mottoes
(or *paroles*) played in strengthening resistance during the war.

But hard and awful, even to death,
And whom He loves, He chasteneth.
In the Garden what was God's reply
Where the Son, in sweat of agony
Lay, pleading long: Let this cup pass? . . .
No word so slimy with the Lie
As this word Love's mendacity. . . .
Is the path narrow, slippery, sheer,
Love teaches them to stop and veer.—
Turn down sin's highway, broad and fair,
Love teaches they need not despair. . . .
They overlook that first the Will
Law's righteous cravings must fulfil. . . .
When Will has won its desperate fight,
Then Love will come into its right . . .
This generation, slack and slow,
Proves Hate the best Love to bestow. . . .
Hate! Hate! [1]

Brand is more than a study in asceticism and the positive
virtues of the fanatic. The hero stands for the principle of
willed renunciation: the last temptation to be overcome is

[1] *Gud's kaerlighed jeg kender til*
og den er ikke vek og mild.
den er til dødens raedsel hård,
den byder klappe så det slår.
Hvad svarte Gud i oljelunden
da sønnen lå i sved og· skraek
og bad og bad: tag kalken vaek! . . .
Ej noget ord blev sølet ned
i løgn som ordet kaerlighed. . . .
Er stien trang og brat og skred,
den knappes af—i kaerlighed!
går en ad syndegaden bred,
han har dog håb—i kaerlighed! . . .
Et springes over: viljen først
må laeske lovens retfaerds-tørst. . . .
Vandt viljen sejr i slig en strid
da kommer kaerlighedens tid. . . .
men her mod slaegten, slap og lad,
ens bedste kaerlighed er had!
Had! Had!

that of the Spirit of Compromise. Brand is therefore a
warrior for truth, but also something of a scourge of God
Orthodoxy would protest that man should not judge his
fellow-men ; the priest may refuse the sacrament to an
unrepentant sinner, the son should have pleaded with his
dying mother.

The dilemma of Love and Judgment, of Righteousness and
Mercy even in the last scene remains a dilemma, since the
Voice which proclaims the God of Love speaks from the
obliterating avalanche.

The hero yet remains a character, not merely an embodied
principle. He is the son of a woman who sacrificed herself
for money and became a miser : on wife and child he lavishes
feelings the more intense that they have no alternate forms.
He has a sardonic humour ; he loves and despises his poor
parishioners (as Swift grew infuriated by the wrongs of the
Irish whilst acutely aware of their shortcomings). He alternates between dry and pawky thrusts at their leader, the Sheriff,
and lyric visions of the True Faith, the coming of Him terrible
as an army with banners. Like Falk, he is swayed between
iconoclasm and idealistic ardour.

Against Brand stands the Sheriff, a shrewd, caustically
humorous Mr. Worldly Wiseman, who plays the rôle that
Guldstad the merchant filled in the earlier play. When Brand
warns the Sheriff that the new doctrine may lead to revolution,
the Sheriff observes that if he is really out for social reform,
Brand had better start some propaganda in the more likely
urban parts.

> Brand : *I have the best : my flock are sure.*
> Sheriff : *Possibly, yes : but I have more* [1]

is the rejoinder and Brand recognizes " the people's champion,"
more dangerous than a worse man, by reason of his doctrine
that social betterment and improved material conditions are
all that matter.

---

[1] Brand : *Min flok er staerk : jeg har de bedste.*
Fogden : *Ja, muligt det : men jeg de fleste.*

Sheriff : *With hostile Nature still our foe*
We've got steam up, and on we go !
Bridges above and roads beneath—
Brand : *But not between our lives and faith.*
Sheriff : *'Twixt fjord and upland cataract.*
Brand : *But not between idea and act.*[1]

The confusion between the spheres of religion and sociology in this play is never finally cleared up, because it is never quite clearly stated nor isolated from the parallel theme of the relation of faith and works. Brand's view is that religion must directly control every act. He does not set his life at a pin's fee ; but insists that all others shall do likewise, and freely denounces those who cannot follow him. There is no future for those who will not drink of the cup ; and the social issue of the Great Disappointment is seen ultimately as an ethical, even a religious issue. The actual references to the Prussian-Danish War are confined to the last scene, but the feeling behind the play is dependent on them. In his final vision of despair, Brand sees his people passing by on the other side with the typical plea of the neutral : "We're a small folk, we."

> *See upon their brows the brand,*
> *" Poor fishers on a barren strand,*
> *Pennypieces of God's mint. . . ."*
> *Not for us the cup He drank,*
> *Not for us the crown of thorn. . . .*[2]

---

[1] Fogden : *Mod trodsende natur i kamp*
er frem vi skredet som med damp !
her brydes vej : her bygges bro—
Brand : *Men ej imellem liv og tro.*
Fogden : *Imellem fjord og viddens sne.*
Brand : *Ej mellem gjerning og idé.*

[2] *Ser dem riste sig på panden*
navn af fattigfolk ved stranden,
folk med skillingspraeg fra Gud. . . .
Ej for os blev kalken drukket,
Ej for os hugg tornekransen. . . .

It is the plea of the Women of Canterbury in T. S. Eliot's
Murder in the Cathedral, a play which in tone and temper is not
unlike *Brand*.[1]

We do not wish anything to happen.
Seven years we have lived quietly,
Succeeded in avoiding notice,
Living, and partly living.
Forgive us, O Lord, we acknowledge ourselves as types of the common
man. . . .

On the other hand Brand's religious despair takes a form
which is partly social, as he envisages Norway smothered in
industrialism, "Britain's smoke-cloud", selling herself for
wealth.[2]

Ibsen himself said at a later date that he was not in this
play concerned with religion as such, and that Brand might
equally well have been an artist or a social reformer.[3] It
is true that Ibsen himself, to whom work was a religion,
might have felt the categorical imperative as strongly as
Brand did. Yet the type of devotion which Brand exemplifies is normally a religious one. Ibsen's model was
Pastor Lammers, and perhaps in writing to Brandes, he may
have been deferring, as usual, to his friend's known suscepti-
bilities.

As a character, Brand convinces, because his pain convinces
—the love for his people, above all the agony of the choice
when he forbears to destroy his wife's ecstasy of renunciation,
though thereby he knows he loses her. The minor characters
are carefully controlled : they are limited but also symbolic,

[1] Brand's tempters are not at all unlike the tempters of St. Thomas, and for
both men temptation comes from the spirit of compromise. But Brand
would not have understood the danger of the Fourth Tempter who offers
the glory of being a martyr, and the power of ruling from the tomb. He
might even have succumbed.

[2] In December 1865, Ibsen wrote to his mother-in-law : " My little boy
shall never, with my consent, belong to a people [i.e. the Norwegians] whose
aim it is to become Englishmen rather than human beings " (Corr., p. 92).

[3] See above, p. 42, note 2.

E

vivid but not particularized.[1] They are indeed characters as another mind might see them from without. The whole play could be conceived of as an internal conflict—as in some of Andreyev's plays—with the hero as the only real character, the others being seen merely in relation to him or standing for aspects of himself. Moreover, unlike Peer, Brand has no moments of relief or relaxation ; his part is all on the top note and so is unactable.

The setting is perhaps more important than the minor characters. It plays its own part in the story, not merely symbolically, in the manner of the heights in *On the Vidda*, but as it really moulded the lives of the people : the isolation, the rigour of winter, the inhuman fastnesses of the fjells and the still living fear of the troll. This kind of country Emily Brontë would have understood. The trolls who assail the hero in the Ice Kirk are neither visions of the mind nor spirits of the heights, but born of the union between the two. It is on the heights that Brand meets his last and worst temptation, and that he lives most completely up to his motto, *All or Nothing*.

Like many of Ibsen's plays, *Brand* in its last act seems to pass into a different realm of being. The lyric *A Church* contains the germ of this act, and reveals more plainly the evil powers intertwined in the very fabric of piety, as the snake and the dove are entwined in Coleridge's *Cristabel*.

> *With toil wrought the King*
> *Through the daylight hours :*
> *Under night's dark wing*
> *Pick and crowbar ring,*
> *Wielded by dark powers. . . .*

---

[1] Agnes, unfortunately, has more than a name in common with Miss Wickfield. In a long speech Brand describes the rôle of comforter and sustainer which is hers, and woman's in general : " He shall strive, attack, endure. She shall deadly deaths wounds cure." Gerd, the troll-girl, is indirectly the fruit of Brand's mother's sin ; for the rejected suitor got her unlawfully in his despair. The Dean is the typical unctuous Churchman ; Ibsen had an unrelenting hostility to the cloth. Einar, artist and convert to sectarianism, is the victim of his own temperament.

The "spire-crown'd kirk" rose "in arrowy pride" with
a "worming troll" as the king's fellow-builder.

> Sunlight or benighted,
> Folk thronged in, 'tis true :
> The bright day unblighted
> To the dark was united :
> They were one, not two.[1]

The power of the trolls of the mountain and the power of
the spirits of the dead are part of Ibsen's Norse inheritance,
and Christianity did not sweep the inheritance away. No
country, not even Ireland, is so filled with legends of ghosts
and dark powers, so haunted with a sense of the other world
as the wilder parts of Norway. Early Norse literature is full
of such legends,[2] and Norse has a richer vocabulary than
English in this particular field. In reading *Brand* or *Ghosts*,
Rosmersholm or any of the later plays it must be remembered
that they are written for a people who had in their
blood, woven into their texture of thinking and feeling, the
legends and dreams that are bred out of lonely living in a
hard land.

4

Peer Gynt's vivacious panorama is the triumph of Ibsen's
early style. The play delighted and annoyed the Norwegians

[1] Kongen han bygged
Dagen lang.
Når natten skygged
Kom troldet og rygged
Med spid og stang . . . .

Døgn-folk flytted
Dog ind i tro :
Thi dags-udbyttet
Til nattens knyttet
Er døgnets jo.

[2] See, e.g., G. D. Kelchner, *Dreams in Old Norse Literature* (Cambridge,
1936), and H. R. Ellis, *The Road to Hel* (Cambridge, 1942).

for the same reasons that Synge's *Playboy of the Western World*
delighted and infuriated the Irish. "She loved him but for
bragging and telling fantastical lies. . . ." This is the raw
material in each case ; but in *Peer Gynt*, trolls and business
men, lunatics in Cairo and idylls in Gudbrandsdal ramify
upon it. Peer, like Christy Mahon, gains freedom when he
stops running away ; but Peer's is a fuller and deeper recovery,
no less than his immortal soul.

Ibsen himself has been quoted for the view that the play
is pure fantasy—what he actually said was that it was capricious.[1] It is kaleidoscopic : the great symbolic scenes—those
with the Trolls and the Button Moulder—carry neither more
nor less of a message than the scenes with Åse or Solveig,
which are pathetic, or those with the tourists and Anitra,
which are comic. The play depends upon the interaction of
all these mutually incompatible modes. It is not a systematic
play because it includes far more of life than can be reduced
to a system, but it has a structure of its own. The episodes
may be capricious but there are none which are irrelevant.
When the play is cut for performance, the omission of familiar
passages brings home the necessity for them. For example,
Peer's successive adventures with Ingrid, the cow-girls, and
the troll Princess form a Rake's Progress, and the cow-girls
are the central link in the group. Peer's descent to the trolls
becomes more sinister if the different steps which lead to it
are marked out.

Peer Gynt is a more serious work than *Ghosts* because it
deals with greater subjects and deals with them more compre-
hensively. It is a far better play than *Brand*, which was
written out of despair, but lacks the clarity of true tragedy.
The story of Peer is the story of his struggle to get away from
the trolls—in Christian phrase, the search for salvation. Peer
is Piers Plowman and Everyman—but he is also a comic
character, a gaily caricatured typical Norwegian ; and finally,
a fairy-tale hero, the troll-slayer of Gudbrandsdal.

Ibsen thought that *Peer Gynt* "will hardly be understood
outside Scandinavia". In his younger days, he had on

---

[1] He also said, "Wine did this ! "

several occasions travelled up the dales collecting folk-lore and stories, and while he was writing the play he immersed himself in Norwegian legends and fairy tales of all kinds. So completely had he thought himself back into Norway that one day as he stood looking at the Italian island of Ischia he said, "Look at that fine hop-garden!" A Danish friend pointed out that he was looking at a vineyard, and Ibsen corrected himself: "Yes, you are right! Now and then I have to pull my own ears to realize I am not in Norway."[1]

The greatness of Peer Gynt lies perhaps most of all in its naivety. Only in a language at once ancient and unworked, only by a people civilized but not urban, could such a reconciliation of moral earnestness and the fantasies of legend be achieved. In Peer Gynt Ibsen was not trying to be " a thinker " —apart from anything else, he wrote the play too quickly for that—but it is based on certitudes, dearly bought and fully acknowledged. The extended perspective which a knowledge of the world beyond had given to Ibsen was turned on material provided by the little world of Norway.

Peer Gynt began his career much as Ibsen began his—a shy country boy ashamed of his poverty, and living on his dreams. His gaucherie lands him in awkward situations, which evoke sudden bursts of real recklessness. At moments he becomes the " mad Norseman ", in a fit of Highland rage or injured pride, and then he dares anything. The setting of moorland and valley, the scenes of peasant life and the characters of these early passages echo those of the poem On the Vidda.[2]

Peer succumbs at once to the shy charms of Solveig, but

[1] Koht, II, p. 9.
[2] The scene where Peer lies in the heather listening to the disparaging remarks of the neighbours reflects section 3 of On the Vidda, where the hero lies in the ling with his own thoughts reproachfully passing " like churchward folk ". Åse, modelled on Ibsen's own mother, recalls the old mother out on the bleaching-square, or in her little hut, singing her child to sleep, with the cat lying beside them. Solveig has something in common with the timid girl, eyes fixed on her shoe-string, whom the hero meets in the summer night. Finally the Strange Hunter has all the acid, accusing sternness of the Button Moulder.

immediately afterwards he smashes up his rival's wedding party and abducts Ingrid the bride. Then in the mountains he becomes the lover of three cow-girls who have already given themselves to the trolls, and from them, he falls to wooing a troll himself. Thus is compassed the Fall of Man.[1]

The troll plays such an important part in Ibsen's work that it is essential to understand him. The troll is not a puck or a goblin ; he is truly diabolic. Although the old stories spoke of monstrous three-headed trolls, the troll may look much like a human being ; only a little stocky, a little malformed. A troll is humanity minus the specifically human qualities ; at once a hideous parody of man and yet only the isolation of his worst potentialities. His likeness to man constitutes his horror and makes him more feared ; he is a cousin of Mr. Hyde with the disgusting imitative faculty of the ape and the baboon. The troll is the animal version of man, the alternative to man : he is also what man fears he may become. Ibsen's use of the troll is more than the invocation of a piece of folk-lore ; it is a poetic mode of stating what could not otherwise be stated except at tedious length, thereby losing its force and becoming another thing.[2]

The trolls belong to the countryside, they are the dwellers on the fjells, but they play much of the part that the devil does in Christian legend. Their motto might be the devil's own—" Troll, to thyself be enough " ; whereas Man carries within a standard of virtue and must be true to himself. Peer submits to all the trolls' habits and customs (much more important than beliefs, as they tell him) ; but when the troll King proposes to get rid of his inconvenient human nature by scratching his eye so that he will ever after see with the eye of a troll, Peer refuses to take such an irrevocable step. He is ready to be a troll on his own terms—and while a way

[1] Peer's wooing of the troll Princess and his adventures with the other trolls seem to be reflected in John's adventures with the brown girl, and other episodes in the early part of Mr. C. S. Lewis's *Pilgrim's Regress*.

[2] The trolls and the " walking dead " are usually substantial figures with great physical powers. Mrs. N. K. Chadwick has recently pointed out the vigour and aggressiveness of Norse ghosts.

out remains. But he finds out first, that he cannot escape :
second, that his desires in the world of trolldom have already
borne fruit (the Biblical reference is obvious) :

Peer : *That lie won't catch you this old trout !*
Green Woman : *You'll be a father before the year's out !* [1]

third, that the trolls are going to kill him for his treachery.
He cries out to his mother ; and immediately the church
bells are heard and he is saved. But Peer escapes only to
be trapped by another troll, the Bøjg. The Bøjg has neither
shape nor form : when Peer asks " Who are you ? " it says,
" Myself." There is nothing to fight : it seems that there
is nothing there at all, but the monstrous invisible troll closes
in and begins to smother him, like a sea-anemone digesting
its prey.

The Great Bøjg wins without a fight. [2]

Peer calls on Solveig : and again he is saved by the bells.
The Bøjg, however, has left him a motto—" Go round about,
Peer." Henceforth his way is to be the way of evasion,
substitution, self-deception. He loves Solveig—but he cannot face her with the troll Princess and her troll child beside
him. [3] Therefore, although he remembers vaguely that the
Bible " says something about repentance ", he leaves Solveig,
who left all for him, disguising cowardice as a feeling that
he is " unworthy " and would soil her, a thought that had
not occurred to him before. After the tender scene of make-
believe with his dying, ruined mother—Peer's very defects
have the grace of virtues lacking in Brand—he goes off to
America—the great solution to all social maladjustments in
the nineteenth century !
  The moral is almost glaringly evident. The trolls might
rub shoulders with the Seven Deadly Sins from *Dr. Faustus*,

[1] Peer : *Du fisker mig ikke med løgnens agn !*
  Den Grønklaedte : *Min Peer, du er faer før året haelder.*
       [2] *Den store Bøjgen vinder uden at kaempe.*
  [3] In his teens, in the unhappy time at Grimstad, Ibsen himself got an
illegitimate child by a servant girl, which he supported for fourteen years.

while the Børg is familiar in accounts of those deep and
deadly temptations which rise from the depths of the mind
itself and ruin a man not for any price at all, but by weight
of inertia as if by pressure of the air around. Yet there is
no deliberate statement of the moral in *Peer Gynt*. In contrast
with *Brand*, it is in this respect truly dramatic ; that is to say,
the implications are at once inescapable and unformulated.
The story runs on its fluid way, and the pattern is worked
out in action. It is worked out, however, in a world which
is seen through the eyes of Peer ; a fairy-tale world in which
inanimate objects come to life, and exciting adventures are
found round every corner.

Peer is a dreamer on such a scale that he can create an
Empire in five minutes from the sands of the desert ; he is
equally ready to bring the Devil or God the Father into his
stories. The merest hint will set him off on a soaring, splendid
flight of fancy ; and the kind of things that happen to him
are like the things he dreams about—even when, as in the
madhouse scene, it is the likeness of parody, or nightmare.
If occasionally he tumbles, it is after a glorious adventure.

And what if I run my ship aground,
Oh, still it was splendid to sail ! [1]

In nothing is Peer more the typical Norwegian than in his
outbursts of fancy. His imagination leads him. It swells and
soars, like the genii coming out of the bottle, or the devil
out of the nut. Peer is a self-intoxicated man. He is a
Dionysiac " with vine leaves in his hair ", he creates his own
world and thus fulfils the troll's motto : " To thyself be—
enough." Peer cannot distinguish between his fancy and fact :
he lives out his dream, even when his mother is dying beside
him. But to label Peer with the labels of the psychologist
as an escapist, as dealing in compensations, or with the labels
of the moral philosopher as deficient in the power of moral
choice, is to be completely irrelevant. It is as futile as asking
whether or not Falstaff is a coward. The whole trend of the

[1] Cf. p. 39.   Peer's enthusiasm is seen ironically however, whilst Falk's
is not.

play implies the inadequacy of such labels. In particular
episodes, Peer's rôle may be straightforward ; but the particular episodes are all interconnected, and the general effect
is far too subtle and complex to be stated in a doctrinaire
fashion. Peer lives by a balance of power : he will not
choose to be anything but himself. If he is cheated by
the tourists or Anitra, forthwith he assumes another rôle.
When he finds that the last metamorphosis crowns him the
Emperor of a madhouse, he is ready to survive even as a
troll, provided only, like Parolles, he may live.

> *Oh, Great One, hold fast !*
> *I am what Thou wilt—a Turk, a sinner,*
> *A Troll : only help me. Something has burst—*
> *I just can't remember the name to call !* [1]

The mutations of the Gyntian Self are finally exposed by
a return to Norway. On the ship he meets the Strange
Passenger, who is Death : and after Death comes the Button
Moulder, who is the Judgment, the Doom. The stages of
Peer's regeneration are threefold. First, he finds his old hut
and hears Solveig singing of himself ; and he realizes that
he has never entered into his rightful kingdom.

> *Ah, anguish, here was my Empire, then.*[2]

His remorse calls up unacted aspirations ; it calls up the
Button Moulder, a figure from his childhood [3] who shows
him that he has not even been a self. " To be one's self is
to slay oneself," and the troll King confirms that Peer has
to himself been *enough*, has been a troll all his life. Finally
the Devil makes the point that Peer has been the wrong sort

---

[1] *Du store—hold fast !*
Jeg er alt, hvad du vil—en Tyrk, en synder—
Et bergtrold—men hjaelp—det var noget, som brast—
Jeg kan ikke hitte dit navn i en hast !
[2] *O, angst ! Her var mit kejserdom !*
[3] Little Peer had often played at casting buttons, as we are told in Act I.
At the auction in Act V the old ladle turns up. The Button Moulder may be
compared with the Rat Wife in *Little Eyolf*, another supernaturally enlarged
reflection of a childhood memory of Ibsen himself.

of self—a negative print. He does not think the catalogue
of Peer's sins worth damnation, and sends Peer back to the
casting ladle. At this point Peer reaches his lowest depths—
he is not fit to exist, he has existed as a mere birth, a natural
product but no more. He lies upon the earth as naked and
despairing as Timon of Athens.

> *Beautiful earth, be not wroth with me*
> *That I trod your fields so uselessly.*
> *Beautiful sun, your rays have shed*
> *Into a cottage untenanted.*
>
> *Beautiful sun and beautiful earth*
> *What folly to nurse her who brought me to birth.*
> *Nature is prodigal, Spirit is scanted.*[1]

At last his sin comes home to him.

> *Round about, said the Bøjg. No—this time*
> *It's straight ahead, were the road ne'er so straitened.*[2]

So he faces Solveig, and finds that his sin is blotted, and
his spiritual human status has been preserved because Solveig
believed in him. She has carried the real Peer in her heart,
as a mother carries a child in her body ; in the last scene,
Solveig succeeds Åse.[3] The wife, or mother, who ignores
all the sin, sees the man as he is—in so far as he is man. The
world knows the troll version. The world says Love is
blind, and so it would appear : but Love overcomes the
world. It is the echo of the Voice that spoke to Brand from

[1] *Du dejlige jord, vaer ikke vred*
At jeg tramped dit graes til ingen nytte.
Du dejlige sol, du har sløset med
Dine lysende staenk i en folketom hytte. . . .
Dejlige sol og dejlige jord
I var dumme, at I bar og lyste for min moer.
Ånden er karrig og naturen er ødsel.
[2] *Udenom sa'e Bøjgen. Nej : denne gang*
tvers igennem, var vejen aldrig så trang !
[3] Peer calls her " My mother ! my wife ! " and as she leans over him
to sing the cradle song she, now old and bent, in her peasant dress, should
recall the earlier figure. This was brought out in Tyrone Guthrie's
production.

the avalanche, given in action, as drama, not exposition.
Solveig singing her cradle song to Peer on the morning of
Pentecost is a naïve picture : it is the "happy-ever-after"
of the fairy story, and it would be overwhelmingly senti-
mental if it were not so strongly controlled. But it is controlled by all that has gone before. Solveig remains enskyed
and sainted in a play where Anitra receives the tribute from
Goethe.[1] The fact that love had literally preserved and
redeemed Peer implies that Solveig saves Peer on quite another
plane from that on which Dr. Wangel saves Ellida, a plane
which the "enlightened" Ibsen did not recognize.

The new quality which enriches *Peer Gynt* above all is
the fullness and richness of ordinary life in it. In Act I and
Act IV the adventures of Peer are merely lively or amusing
or scandalous, like the adventures of Faustus between the sale
of his soul and the hour of damnation—a necessary interlude
but an interlude by definition. In this sense it is true that
much of *Peer Gynt* is capricious, an exuberant comic caprice,
a sort of Twelfth Night revel. The delicious inconsistencies
of Åse in pursuit of her runaway—

> *I wish he would fall and . . .*
> *Tread carefully up there now !* [2]

the unassailable buoyancy of Peer, who, when he has been
promising Anitra a soul, and she tells him she would prefer
an opal, is enraptured by her faithfulness to type instead of
being dashed by her lack of attention to what he is saying—
the gay nonsense of the Devil's last words as he goes off to
look for Peer at the Cape of Good Hope, sent by the sinner
in question—

---

[1] *Anitra ! you're one of Eve's genuine daughters,*
Magnetically charming me—for I'm a man.
And as a respected old buffer has told us,
"Das ewige weibliche zieht uns an !"

Anitra ! Evas naturlige datter !
Magnetisk jeg drages : thi jeg er mand
og som der står hos en agtet forfatter ;
"Das ewige weibliche zieht uns an !"

[2] *O gid du faldt ned og . . .!*
Traed varsomt i haeldet !

62

IBSEN THE NORWEGIAN

The Cape, O the Cape. it always defeats me—
There are heaps of such terrible Stavanger missionaries.[1]

these are perhaps unrelated to the main issue by any strict
logic. Yet they are all digested into the play, along with
the minor characters, the lunatics, the sailors, the cook, the
mutilated peasant, the thief and receiver.[2]

Ibsen's language is the solvent—easy, strong, packed with
images, legends, scenes and customs of Norway. Only with
that background could Ibsen, writing in the stuffy 'sixties,
have started from the fairy-tale level. If he had belonged
to one of the great nations, like William Morris, he could
have cultivated simplicity and robustness : he would not
have been able to take them for granted. It was his peculiar
happy medium which allowed him at one moment to be
expounding " Whosoever will lose his life shall save it " and
the next moment to be indulging in broad farce. The world
of *Peer Gynt* is a freer and more spacious world than the
interior of the Doll's House, or even the Romsdal of the
last plays. Although his later reputation as a sort of Jeremiah
of the Enlightenment was certainly a libel and singularly
obnoxious to Ibsen, he never regained the vivacity and scope
of *Peer Gynt*. He gave them up for a narrower, intenser
and more rigid form.

Peer Gynt is a greater work than *Ghosts*, but it could never
be called a greater play. Like *Brand* it is described as a
dramatic poem, and was written without reference to the
stage. The hero again dominates the action completely—
James Agate observed that Peer is always on the stage and

---

[1] *Det Kapland, det Kapland var mig altid imod—*
der findes nogle slemme missionaerer fra Stavanger.

[2] Thief : *My father stole,*
   His son must steal.
Receiver : *My father received,*
   His son must receive.

Tyvan : *Min fader var tyv*
   hans søn må stjaele.
Haeleren : *Min fader var haeler :*
   hans søn må haele.

A drastically deterministic doctrine of the self !

always talking—and Ibsen's poetry really made the producer's efforts unnecessary. The Bojg has been presented in the verse itself, and any stage presentation must be supplementary. Above all, the great moments of the drama do not depend on stage presentation, because there is no dramatic clash between character and character, no sudden tightening or relaxing of the tension. There is nothing like the entry of Nora in her outdoor clothes, or the moment when Mrs. Alving and Pastor Manders hear the whispers from the dining room. *Peer Gynt* has none of those particular virtues which the Ibsenites delighted in, and which are set out in *The Old Drama and the New*.

Chapter Three

THE MORALIST

" Emperor and Galilean "—" The League of Youth "
" Pillars of Society "—" A Doll's House "
" Ghosts "—"An Enemy of the People "

*B*RAND and *Peer Gynt* had been poured out at top speed.
The second *Brand* had been written in six months : and
after it " *Peer Gynt* came as though of itself ".[1]   The sequel was
that Ibsen sat down and brooded for six years on the compos-
ition of a long, extremely dull drama in two parts on the
subject of Julian the Apostate.   He himself regarded it as the
greatest of his works, the one which set forth his life's-philos-
ophy most completely.   No critic has ever agreed with him.

There is no doubt that this monstrous production was of
the greatest significance for Ibsen personally.   It is heavy
with something which is never completely brought to light
—as Mr. Eliot said of *Hamlet*.   Ibsen begins by a very sympathetic attitude to Julian, and ends up by departing from
historical fact in order to discredit him—much to the bewilderment of Archer who felt that Julian, as an enlightened
agnostic, deserved more respectful treatment.   The play is
Ibsen's one attempt to be a thinker, and it shows how little
he was fitted to dabble in theorizing, though it was written,
re-written and finally cut down from three parts to two.
Curiously enough, part of this vision of the Tredje Rige,
the Third Reich, was written at Berchtesgaden.

The first part, *Cæsar's Apostacy*, is a melodrama, with
Julian as a decadent, brilliant youth, the lover of Helena,
the too-successful general—a play of intrigue with a decor-
ative historical setting.   Ibsen had archæologized for this play
much as he did for his nationalist historical plays ; but as
he now regarded himself as emancipated from nationalism

[1] *Corr.*, p. 200.

he went back to the Roman Empire. *The Emperor Julian* is a study in degeneration, and it makes a single strong effect, but one which is not clear-cut. There is none of the intrigue of Part I, but a vaguely-defined cumulative emotional movement. Julian grows steadily more tyrannical, more deluded, till he is cheated with a prophecy about "the Phrygian regions"—rather in the manner of *Macbeth*—and dies in battle, to be succeeded by the Christian Jovian. Yet his love for Beauty, his Bacchic vision, revives at the end, recalling that earlier scene where with his procession of revellers he appeared as the priest of Dionysus, "with vine leaves in his hair", opposing the martyrs' ecstatic procession to the arena.

Both plays are provided with a *raisonneur*, Maximus the Mystic, who stages a kind of Witches' Scene of Cain and Judas feasting with Julian, the third Scourge of God, pre-destined by the World-Will to a career of crime. Schopenhauer finally gave way to Hegel in the third kingdom, foreshadowed by Maximus' prophecy, which was to combine Hebraism and Hellanism—as Heine would have said—into something higher and holier far.

Maximus: The World-Will shall give a reckoning for Julian's soul.

Basil: Blaspheme not: verily hast thou loved the dead, but——

Maximus: Loved and betrayed him!—No, not I—he was betrayed like Cain—betrayed like Judas. Your God is a spendthrift God, Galilean! He squanders many a soul!— Wert thou not this time the destined man—thou sacrifice to Necessity? What then is it worth to have lived? All is a game and a jest—even to will is to have been forced to will! Oh, my beloved, all signs deceived me, all omens spoke with double sense, so that I truly thought thee the reconciling power of the Two Kingdoms.

The Third Kingdom shall come! The soul of man shall come into its own at last, and then shall men offer sacrifice for thee and thy two guests in the symposium!

This fit of Teutonic dogmatizing seemed to be driving Ibsen further from the stage. *Brand* and *Peer Gynt* can be acted, though little is gained by doing so. In this work, however, Ibsen had evidently no idea of a performance.[1]

He insisted again that the material had been provided by his own experience, and that the play represented a new phase in his intellectual development.

> *Emperor and Galilean* is the first work which I wrote under German intellectual influence. . . . My view of life was still that of a Scandinavian nationalist. . . . I was in Germany during the war (of 1870) and the development consequent upon it. All this acted in many ways upon me with the force of a transforming power. My theory of history and of human life had till then been a national one : now it expanded into a racial theory and I could write *Emperor and Galilean*.[2]

This deplorable statement shows clearly that Ibsen was winding himself into a cocoon of Germanic verbiage. Theories of human life (save the mark !) were all too common ; of " the racial theory " fortunately little seems to have survived in his work. But the influence of Schopenhauer was deep and lasting. The World-Will enthroned in blindness over a predetermined creation was a nightmare which was to haunt Ibsen. He saw humanity as tiny figures caught in an evolutionary machine. Nature—or God—is a spendthrift, to whom the death of millions means little.

Very indirectly it can be seen that the play is connected with Ibsen's own personal conflict between the ascetic and the Dionysiac, between Brand and Peer Gynt. He himself had an artist's love of life and an artist's sensuousness, but he sacrificed them to his work. Julian denies the necessity of the sacrifice, and tries to find a middle way : but he is defeated. It cannot be said that the personal equation here gives the play any added interest.

It may be that *Emperor and Galilean* is the defiance of God which Solness describes in a later play, in a passage which is generally read as autobiographical. The Master Builder accused his Creator of taking away all human happiness from

[1] It was not performed till 1896 when a German theatre staged it. This attempt has never been repeated.

[2] *Corr.*, pp. 413-4.

him to make him a better artist, and in his turn threatened
to build no more churches for such a God. *Emperor and
Galilean* shows the utter waste of a human life—for which the
World-Will, although not a Person, is clearly held responsible.
It exemplifies the favourite nineteenth-century sport of
scolding God for His failure to come up to what Man expects
of Him. Ibsen never spoke out directly on this subject, but
it seems clear that the work of Strauss and his followers had
broken down his faith. His friendship with Brandes, a Jew
turned free-thinker, and his growing alienation from Bjørnson
are symptomatic of such a change.

In *Brand* and *Peer Gynt*, the religious issue had been in the
centre of the picture—an undogmatic but a deeply personal
religion, of the kind which Pastor Lammers had been preaching
at Skien. Even in *On the Vidda* God had made a rather
unexpected appearance in the last stanza. If in his first misery
after the Great Disappointment, Ibsen had turned to religion,
and to the particularly personal and inward religion which
the disciples of Kierkegaard were propagating, his encounter
with the Higher Criticism and the theories of the Germans
must have dealt him a second blow more severe than the
first, although from the nature of the case, the evidence
would not be clear in his writings. It seems possible that
the ten years' silence in Germany, and the new and drastic
change which came over his work were due to the loss of
faith, and that the despair which can be felt behind the confusion of *Emperor and Galilean* was for a time such as to make
writing impossible. In all his other plays, Ibsen wrote about
things of which he knew, which he had seen—literally, as
well as with his mind's eye. The settings of *Peer Gynt*, for
example, are limited to Norway and Africa—though he did
not visit Egypt till some years later. The reason for his
choice of story in *Emperor and Galilean* he never explained ;
it had been long in his mind and may even date from Bergen
days. The play remains a cryptic witness to the stress through
which Ibsen passed ; having written it, he maintained silence
for a further period of four years, until the production of
Pillars of Society in 1877.

F

2

Whilst he was writing the World-Historical Drama Ibsen broke off to produce a five-act comedy, *The League of Youth* (1869). Eight years later he produced a four-act drama, *Pillars of Society* (1877). These two plays are the only fruits of the ten years spent in Germany. The next year he returned to Rome, and within a twelvemonth had written *A Doll's House*.

The ten barren years in Germany between Ibsen's fortieth and fiftieth years were a period of incubation. Whilst on the surface he was fully absorbed in his unwieldy philosophic drama, the deeper currents of his mind are shown in these shorter plays. They should not be looked on merely as first exercises in " social drama ". They are social comedies in a special sense, studies in local colour, in the foibles of a particular social group, the lords of parish-pump politics, the shapers of *lokale forholde*. These two plays are not concerned with the inner life at all ; their purpose is not to point a general truth or expound universal problems, as Ibsen happily imagined himself to be doing in *Emperor and Galilean*. Here he is merely having a few private words with his compatriots about their own particular shortcomings. He referred to *The League of Youth* as " this peaceable play " but the Norwegians did not share that view of it. When it was put on, there were riots at the theatre, and the warfare between the Young Party and Ibsen's supporters went on for some time. Ibsen was in Egypt, representing Norway at the celebration for the opening of the Suez Canal. He wrote a satiric poem, *From Port Said*, in which he said merely :

My home's still the old home, I see !

The Young Party, the progressive group in Norway, felt this play as black treachery and Bjørnson, who thought that he was the original of Stensgård, spoke of " assassination in the groves of poesy ". But as the hubbub died down the Norwegians began to appreciate the joke. *The League of Youth* has held the stage in Norway ; but it is a family joke and the outside world has not appreciated it.

The Ibsenites have pointed out that this is Ibsen's first prose comedy—it is indeed the first prose comedy in Norwegian—and that it is well constructed according to the school of Scribe ; that Selma the girl-wife who is treated as a doll is a first sketch for Nora, and that the forged bankbill used for blackmailing is also a foretaste of *A Doll's House*. At best, however, they can only regard it as " an experimental, transitional work, in which the poet is trying his tools "[1] though admittedly " very amusing on the stage ".

Such was Ibsen's modest ambition. He was *trying* to be funny. Archer observed sadly that when Mrs. Rundholmen mistakes Stensgård's overtures on behalf of Bastien for a proposal, " We are irresistibly reminded of Mrs. Bardell's fatal misunderstanding of Mr. Pickwick's intentions." Precisely. Mrs. Rundholmen and Mrs. Bardell would have been capital friends, and Stensgård would have recognized a kindred spirit in Mr. Alfred Jingle, whisking off the spinster aunt—with the money borrowed from Tracy Tupman—in a fast postchaise and four.

Stensgård has been called Peer Gynt in politics. He has indeed Peer Gynt's fluency and his conviction that Providence has not only destined him for greatness but is prepared specially to intervene on his behalf. But whereas Peer Gynt is seen from the inside, Stensgård is presented only from the outside. Stensgård storming at Fjeldbo's hint of caution is a creature who does not soliloquize (a fact in which his creator took some professional pride) and who could not soliloquize. What distinguishes him is his hypersensitive response to encouragement, his inflammable resentment of imaginary slights. He lives only on the adulation or approbation of others. He is essentially a social parasite.

> You are my enemy [he upbraids Fjeldbo]. You have always been my enemy. Just look around and see how everyone else appreciates me, stranger as I am. You, on the other hand, you who know me, have never appreciated me. That is the radical weakness of your character. . . .

[1] Archer, preface to *The League of Youth*. *Collected Works*, VI, p. xi.

"Am I fit for nothing?" asks Fjeldbo drily and Stensgård superbly retorts : "Have you ever been fit to appreciate ME?"

> Oh, isn't it unspeakable joy [he cries on another occasion] to carry all that multitude away and along with you? How can you help becoming good from mere gratitude? And how it makes you love all your fellow creatures! I feel as if I could clasp them all in one embrace, and weep, and ask their forgiveness because God has been so partial to give me more than them!

To accuse Stensgård of jobbery is like accusing Falstaff of blarney or Figaro of lying. It is confounding a master of his craft with petty practitioners. When he hands back the forged bill, now useless to him, with the grand gesture : "That is how I treat men who vote against me!" our pleasure is in the consciously immoral joy of watching him get away with it.

The other characters nobly support Stensgård. Chamberlain Bratsberg is a benevolent despot, a little bewildered by the antics of the younger generation, but full of fire and activity for a righteous cause. His farewell to Stensgård might be modelled on Mr. Pickwick's farewell to Messrs. Dodson and Fogg. Aslaksen and Heire are humours of the Dickensian sort—easy meat for any actor of experience. Both are modelled from the life—Aslaksen from the printer who had set up the political paper to which Ibsen in his early youth contributed, and Heire from Ibsen's own father. But they must have been nearer caricatures than portraits.

The well-worn tricks of comedy are the natural groundwork of the play—the substituted letter, the overheard conversations, the four pairs of lovers who "set to partners". Experience teaches economy in their use : here there are rather too many of them. They perform the same duty as the bone supporters with which the ladies of the period stiffened their bodices. The stuff to be stiffened is the *lokale forholde*. Unfortunately for the English reader, a knowledge of Norwegian ways is taken for granted, and the play is therefore as difficult for a foreigner as one of Emlyn Williams or Sean O'Casey. The exact social standing of Bratsberg, Momsen and Lundestad, the position of Heire, the extent to which Mrs. Rundholmen and Aslaksen are part of the *lokale forholde* are complicated matters of which no explanation is given because the requisite knowledge is assumed. In a small town of about 2,000 inhabitants the local magnate is a very great man ; but the local printer has also to be considered, especially at election time, and especially where local politics are the only politics that count, and form the best indoor sport for all but the very young. Even today, in the remoter parts of Norway, the question of a new road or a new port of call for the steamer, the election of the burgomaster, or the local council will rouse everyone to battle, when a question of national policy will hardly touch them at all. In a country so large and thinly inhabited, without large industrial interests or a National Press, and with a tradition of local government that is stronger and older than the national tradition, it is inevitable that the emphasis should be on district affairs.[1] In the nineteenth century when foreign politics were still a matter for Stockholm, and when Norway was so much more cut off from the rest of Europe, narrower horizons were imposed. If *The League of Youth* is read, not as a contribution to sociology but as the Norwegian equivalent of one of the Abbey Theatre productions, it still has life.

3

Ibsen said of *The Pillars of Society* : " It may in a manner be regarded as the counterpart of *The League of Youth* : it will enter pretty thoroughly into several of the more im-

---

[1] The natural unit of government in Norway is the *thing*, the local assembly. Its English equivalent, the shire-moot, has only attained comparable significance in the case of the L.C.C. In England, easier communications soon made the Parliament the chosen instrument of government. In Norway the Storthing has many of the constitutional powers of Parliament but it has not its traditional authority. The tragic implications of this local patriotism are the material of the earlier play *Kingmaking* (see above, p. 23).

portant questions of the day."[1]   In fact the play is the Un-
peaceable or Unpleasant counterpart of the Peaceable and
Pleasant *League of Youth*.   Yet it was received with enthusiasm.
Ibsen's way had perhaps been prepared for him by the social
plays of Bjørnson, which had come out in the previous few
years.[2]

In this play something of the method of his later work
is applied to the material of *Peer Gynt* and *The League of
Youth*. The play depicts Grimstad, the town where Ibsen
had spent six years as an underdog, and whose respectable
citizens he had fiercely lampooned. Contemporary excitement over Plimsoll's reforms, contemporary scandals about
the New Woman may be worked into the structure : the
groundwork is the life of the intensely respectable little clique
who run the town and of whom Bernick is the leader, and
who with their equally respectable women folk are collec-
tively as well as individually indicted. This is the argument
of the play, and there is some offence in it.

The plot is again too crammed with incident. The satire on
business methods, local politics, the interlude of the foreman
with its implications on capital and labour, the story of Lona
Hessel, the love of John and Dina, Dina's own history, the
adventure of little Olaf, with its surprising forecast of the
story of Little Eyolf,[3] the stories of Martha and of Mrs.
Bernick would overcrowd the canvas even without the main
story, that of the Consul himself. The "important questions
of the day" which are touched are two—the danger of commercialism and the revolt of the women. Bernick is a
variation upon that familiar character in Ibsen, the strong
man who lives for his work. He has something of Brand,
something of Solness, more perhaps of Borkman. Like
Borkman he gives up his real love and oversteps the law for
the sake of "the power and the glory". Unlike Borkman,

---

[1] *Corr.*, p. 291.

[2] *The Bankrupt*, written three years before *Pillars of Society*, has as its hero
a public figure who tries to cover up his difficulties by dubious means, but
is converted in the end.

[3] The likeness extends even to the father's final exclamation—" I can see
that the boy has never really belonged to me."

he repents ; but Bernick's repentance is a dramatic conven-
ience ; it allows him to become the *raisonneur* and expound
the moral of the play. No other end would be appropriate
—the play is not written in a tragic mood and the social
comedy of Act I could never have been associated with a
wholesale slaughter of the innocents aboard the *Indian Girl*.
Nevertheless, Bernick's faults are not the kind to make a
conversion plausible. The ne'er-do-well may reform, the
religious fanatic may melt, but the business man does not
lean up against the wall and grow generous, even under the
shock of narrowly averted child-murder. His repentance is
in tune with the play as a whole ; but out of tune with his
own past story.

The revolt of the women is a theme which is divided
among the four women characters. Dina, Lona, Betty and
Martha have each their private story, but for all of them the
issue is the same—shall they stagnate, or shall they free themselves, at the risk of becoming unwomanly ? Lona and Dina
choose freedom : Betty and Martha choose sacrifice. They
are not condemned ; Martha is an almost Tchekovian figure,
who is content to resign her lover to the young girl whom
she has brought up and grown to love also.

Ibsen's growing power as a dramatist is found not in the
problems nor in the characters, but in the detail, in the new
method of construction by means of interplay. It is the sum
of these tiny links which really makes the structure. The
play is built up, not hewn out. It has the firmness, not of
plate armour, but of chain mail. Because Ibsen was not yet
practised in this method, it was necessary for him to have a
large number of characters each dependent on one another
but each aiming at different things. The dramatic effect
depends upon the different lines of interest converging and
suddenly reacting upon each other. The sailing of the *Indian
Girl* is the climax of Aune's, Betty's and Bernick's stories,
which are so intertwined that the decision of Aune—a very
minor character—constitutes the final dénouement : he " takes
it on himself" to stop the coffin-ship, at Betty's request. The
whole movement is so finely adjusted that a slight shift any-

where alters the whole situation, and the interest of the play lies largely in seeing how a perfectly simple and ordinary decision by one person can have effects undreamed of upon the others.   Such construction must be planned to the last detail ; the writing must give the impression that events are proceeding in a natural way, yet in each case dissection must show that a word, a movement, a gesture were sending out ripples all round, slightly modifying all the course of events for all the characters.   The danger of the method is that it should end in clockwork ingenuity, leaving the play an animated automaton.   In a detective story, the innocent surface of events covers all the implications and clues that are unfolded in the final chapter.   But the " mechanic beauties ", as Dryden would have called them, are in themselves a temptation : they harden and isolate the " story " from the " treatment " and the bones of the plot are overlaid with an artificial style, instead of being organically at one with it.   In a few great writers, the style itself being one of ironic implication has naturally worked out both in detail and general structure in terms of interplay.   This gives a wonderfully close, intricate and satisfying texture, because the large-scale planning and the finest detail are turned out of the same mould.   It involves in the artist both a love of minutiæ and fine finish, and a sense of proportion and scale, so that the detail is not overworked.   Construction through interplay is best exemplified in English in the later novels of Jane Austen.

A chance remark of Miss Bates, a slight resemblance between Edmund and Sir Thomas Bertram—their common habit of referring punctually to their watch for example—is both local and general in its effect.   For in *Emma* the indirect and glancing play of social intercourse upon firmly moulded characters is the structural basis of the book, which is concerned, much as Ibsen is, with *lokale forholde*.   And in *Mansfield Park* the submerged and powerful pull of family life, the likenesses and differences between kin—which were the main interest of Jane Austen's own life—constitute the groundwork. Edmund's likeness to his father, his solemn conscientiousness, so youthful, so thick-headed and so kind-hearted, marks him

out as the predestined victim of Miss Crawford's wiles and
the object of Fanny's blind veneration. But Edmund's
character is built up by a series of delicate hints, such as his
unlucky habit of testing Miss Crawford's statements in the
wilderness at Sotherton by pulling out a timepiece : it is
dramatically done. We are never given a direct statement,
an explanation of Edmund.

Jane Austen was both mistress of her little world and part
of it : she was detached yet absorbed in the happy provincial-
ism of the day. Ibsen too had detached himself with some
violence from his little world : but now, after an interval,
he was becoming absorbed again—not in the passionate
manner of *Love's Comedy* and *Brand*, not even in the polemical
manner of the poem that he wrote at the same time as this
play (*Langt Borte*, or *From Far Away*) but with a cooler, a
more professional attention. The rottenness of society is
introduced by the conversation of the ladies at the tea-party ;
but how much more gently than in *Love's Comedy* ! The
pastor here is not, like Pastor Stråmand, a figure of fun with
his moment of pathos ; he is a sycophant exposed without
excitement but without mercy.

Ibsen worked over and over the material for this play,
rewriting, revising, always paring down, sharpening and filing
to a nicer point. Here, as in the plays to follow, it is the
final revision which counts. The individual strokes, telling
as they are, are dependent on their placing ; the whole effect
is due to the consistency and evenness of the work. If implication and interplay are to be the method, it is impossible
to let them appear in patches. If irony is not sustained, it
becomes meaningless.

In this play Ibsen did not quite achieve perfect consistency,
but he is well on the way to it. Some speeches are a little
too coloured by the " problem ", insufficiently dramatic, or
out of character.[1] *Pillars of Society* looks back to *Love's*

---

[1] The recantation of Bernick has already been mentioned. Another
example is the final resolve of Dina to put emancipation before matrimony,
in her plans for life in America. The justifications of Aune are a third
example.

Comedy as well as anticipating *A Doll's House*, which followed in the short space of two years and finally established Ibsen as the greatest dramatist of his day.

In one respect, the " problems " of *Pillars of Society* forecast developments which were to come much later in Ibsen's writing ; that is, in the stress on the conflict between old and young. The older generation in the person of Lona Hessel revolt from sheer force of temperament, without the support of a creed, throw up their caps and shout, " Up the rebels ! " while Dina's generation go forth with a programme and a mission.

In themselves, however, the characters in this play are not particularly interesting. Their interest depends only on their place in the plot. There is no unexpected yet inevitable development, no sudden moment which defines and gathers up the significance of the part. Variety replaces concentration. The contrast with *The League of Youth* is not more striking than the contrast with the play to follow.

4

A Doll's House almost irresistibly invites sweeping generalizations. It is the first Modern Tragedy, as Ibsen originally named it. The strong divorce play and the social drama are alike descended from it. *A Doll's House* stands in relation to modern drama as Queen Victoria to the royal families of Europe. It is not Ibsen's greatest play, but it is probably his most striking achievement, in the sense that it changed most decisively the course of literature. Its significance for contemporaries is quite distinct from its permanent significance or, again, from its place in the personal development of Ibsen as an artist.

In the usual manner of the great innovators Ibsen took the conventions of the day and adapted them for his own ends. In *A Doll's House* he is indebted for some of the tricks of the trade to the *pièce bien faite*, the French drama of Scribe and his school, which had formed the staple fare at the Oslo and Bergen theatres when Ibsen was producing there.

France still led the theatrical world. Her critics provided judgments and standards ; but her dramatists were for the most part efficient journeymen. Nevertheless, the *pièce bien faite* has been unfairly despised. It abounded in conventions where the regular puppets—heavy father, innocence distressed, rough diamond, jealous husband, faithful friend—underwent the usual trials—mistaken identity, lost letter, guilty secret, sealed lips—leading to the final pistol shot or the final embrace. Their technique, as efficient as that of a detective story, gave these plays the precision of clockwork toys ; they were topped off with some little moral platitude which would command uncritical assent. They did not pretend to be literature. Literature was left to the long-winded poets of the historical drama, with their five acts on Mary Queen of Scots or Jeanne d'Arc. The main energy of the stage went into experiments with gas lighting, costume and effects—the tradition which later brought real pigs and real trees on the stage of the *Théâtre Libre*. In France there was a genuinely experimental spirit in production, which found its leader in Antoine. In England, unfortunately, the interest in staging took the grosser form of a liking for spectacle for its own sake. Adaptations of Dickens and Scott gave the managers of Drury Lane and Covent Garden full scope. Mediocrities like Tom Taylor turned out plays by the hundred. Poets like Swinburne wrote their unactable poetic dramas, emphasizing the divorce between literature and the stage.[1]

Nevertheless, the nineteenth century saw European literature again becoming a unit, as it had been in the Middle Ages. National dramatic traditions broke down under the more rapid exchange of ideas, of technical developments, and of social habit. Even in countries where the national tradition was strong and healthy, as in Russia, it was modified by the theatrical developments taking place elsewhere.

Ibsen's own reputation was the fruit of this new cosmopolitanism. He was the first, and perhaps the only writer to

[1] See *The Victorian Drama*, by Ernest Reynolds (Heffer and Sons, 1937).

achieve as a dramatist the kind of European fame which now belongs to film stars.[1] The nineteenth century dramatic tradition *is* Ibsen : and Ibsen for many years, and to some people even today, means the author of *A Doll's House*.

His transformation appears so simple now. He had written in the style of the *pièce bien faite* as early as *Lady Inger*, which is modelled on Scribe. He took those parts of the technique which made for clear, forcible presentation and subjected them to the pressure of his personal technique of interplay and implication. This produced a new kind of drama, peculiarly incisive, and when the material was the great question of the day the result was explosive. It took ten years for the effects to be felt in England, but Shaw's *Quintessence of Ibsenism* records the impact.[2] The Ibsenites were not interested in literature as such : they left such interest to the Decadents. To them, Ibsen was above all " a great moral teacher ". The original plays were unknown, and the current translations would have defied the power of Mrs. Siddons. Granville Barker once offered a prize to anyone who could put across Nora's last words as rendered by one enthusiast : " That the miracle of miracles should come to pass—that a combination between us should be a marriage."

The literature of one's youth is a revelation in a way that no later masterpieces can ever be. It was the young who saluted Ibsen, as the young of the nineteen-twenties saluted D. H. Lawrence, and the young of the nineteen-thirties W. H. Auden. They saw great writing in these caricatures of translations, emancipating themselves with a Roundhead zeal and sternness. In that golden age ideologies flourished. The Decadents, no less than those who followed Mr. Gladstone in reading *Robert Elsmere*, were passionate for their creed. Ibsen created such a stir as nowadays no writer could hope for. "Dramatic impotence, ludicrous amateurishness, nastiness, vulgarity, egotism, coarseness, absurdity, uninteresting verbosity [!], suburbanity ! " cried the *Daily Telegraph*, and Shaw replied :

[1] Ibsen became so fashionable that cigarettes, coffee and clothes were advertised as being " à la Ibsen ".   [2] Written in 1891.

Shakespear had put ourselves on the stage but not our situations. . . . Ibsen supplies the want left by Shakespear. He gives us not only ourselves but our situations. The things that happen to his stage figures are things that happen to us. One consequence is that his plays are much more important to us than Shakespear's. Another is that they are capable both of hurting us cruelly and of filling us with excited hopes of escape from idealistic tyrannies and with visions of intenser life in the future.[1]

This is how every generation of youth sees its prophets, Auden, Lawrence, or Ibsen. "Bliss was it in that dawn to be alive!" But the colours fade and for the next generation the enthusiasm becomes inexplicable. Ibsen might have written something as perishable as Godwin's *Political Justice*, and still have made a name. But though it was not recognized, and was, perhaps, not at the time a deciding factor, his achievement was literary and to that extent permanent. Had he united the high seriousness of Mrs. Humphry Ward to the technical dexterity of Conan Doyle this would suffice his international admirers, who ignored the true basis of the play's greatness—a style in which each speech was interlocked by implication to the total structure of the play, an organization as close and exact as that of the most elaborate verse, and perhaps only possible to one who for nearly twenty years had thought and written as a poet.

Now that Nora's situations are sixty-five years behind the times, *A Doll's House* has for some people only the exasperating stamina of indestructible craftsmanship lavished on obsolete material—like an old horsehair sofa that *will* not wear out, and is banished from nursery to attic, given away to the housemaid's mother and turns up in the junk shop, together with the coloured picture of the Jubilee, and the flower pot shaped like a white china swan. The hard staring outlines of the minor characters, the conventional tricks of the letter box and the tarantella seem as primitive as the sense of "duty towards myself" which provokes Nora not only to slam the door but—an unlettered girl, unschooled, unpractised—to wave

[1] *Quintessence of Ibsenism* (p. 144).

every banner in the cause of enlightenment from Agnosticism to Anarchism.

A Doll's House is certainly the least Norwegian of Ibsen's plays. By comparison with England or France, Norway had no city life, and very little of that taint of commercialism which pushed women into the peculiarly humiliating position of being completely dependent on the wage-earning male, without sharing in the breadwinning as the woman in an agricultural or fishing community must do. Perhaps rootlessness and irresponsibility were recognized so clearly because they were so alien ; and there is still probably less suburbia in Norway than in any other country of Western Europe.

In earlier ages it had been felt that

> *God's universal law*
> *Gave to the man despotic power*
> *Over his female in due awe,*

but this had not excluded woman from supremacy in her own recognized domains. In the nineteenth century the subjection was the more irksome because it was less defined, less a social than a personal exercise of the power of material coercion, in short not a rule of law but a despotism. The head of a household might, like Mr. Barrett of Wimpole Street, be unaware of the basis of his action, which could be refined to an intolerable intensity through the structure of Victorian " family-life "—that is to say, life centred round the family not as a functional economic unit but as an economic dependency, subject to the " head of the house ". Subtle and increasing powers of sensibility—all the development of the personal, private consciousness which is represented by the Romantic movement in literature—put new weapons into the hands of the Tyrant Man. Fanny Burney was a woman of acute sensibility but she probably did not suffer from the social tyranny of the Court—she did not have the capacity for suffering—as Elizabeth Barrett did from the tyranny of her father.

The situation was sensed long before it was attacked by the pioneers of Women's Rights. It was described often

enough by Dickens, the more powerfully because usually
without any social *arrière pensée*. In his last work, *The Mystery
of Edwin Drood* (1870), written only nine years before *A Doll's
House*, the epitaph on Mrs. Sapsea sets out an ideal of wifely
reverence which is expounded at greater length but in all
seriousness in such a popular work as *Within the Maze*. [1]
A Doll's House is the Norwegian version of the great theme
of later nineteenth century literature throughout Europe, the
sufferings of women in a masculine world : the theme of
Anna Karenina, and *Madame Bovary*, of *The Egoist*, *Tess of the
D'Urbervilles* and *Portrait of a Lady*.

Ibsen and Tolstoy were incomparably the greatest literary
figures of their time, and produced their greatest work when
this matter was just sufficiently recognised for literary treatment. Ibsen expressed his disapproval of John Stuart Mill's
Subjection of Women, saying, à propos of the Englishman's
contention that his wife had inspired all he wrote, that it
would be a pretty thing not to know whether to be indebted
to Mr. or Mrs. Mill for a literary masterpiece ! But he was
clearly affected by the same mental climate as Mill. Tolstoy
could be scarcely said to inhabit the same climate as these
two, yet in comparing *A Doll's House* with *Anna Karenina*,
which had appeared only six years earlier, the differences of
approach, of method, of language and of structure cannot
obscure the likenesses between these great works in their
fundamental assumptions. Both are concerned with the
deeper aspects of the conflict between two worlds—the
woman's world of personal relationships and human values
against the man's world of legal rights and duties—Isobel
against Angelo, Portia against the laws of Venice.

Pay thrice his money and deface the bond !

Time has been kinder to Tolstoy than to Ibsen, whose fine

[1] By Mrs. Henry Wood (1872). The epitaph reads : *Ethelinda* | Rever-
ential Wife of | THOMAS SAPSEA | AUCTIONEER, ESTATE AGENT, VALUER, ETC. |
of this City | Whose Knowledge of the World | Though somewhat Extensive |
Never brought him acquainted with | *A spirit* | More capable of | *Looking
up to him.* | *Stranger, Pause,* | And ask thyself the Question | *Canst thou Do
Likewise ?* | If not, | *With a Blush, Retire.*

hard style looks like an etching tool after Tolstoy's brimming palette.   In Tolstoy the qualities of the novel as a *genre* are perfected ;   the structure is effected by broad groupings and relief ;   innumerable resolved contrasts of detail are there, but the flavour of each moment is preserved full and clear.   This richness of experience, where the imperceptible gradations of time work stealthily yet inevitably to transform Anna from the reigning beauty to the poor crazed suicide are far more congenial to the modern temper than Ibsen's rigid patterns. Book I of *Anna Karenina*, for example, closes with Anna's ravelled history at that point where she leaves her husband, and begins her descent to death.   Book II opens with the stately Orthodox wedding of Kitty and Levine.   The one story is delicate and subtly told, the other is more broadly and boldly handled, yet there are all the time not two stories but one novel in which both are included.   Tolstoy works by assimilation, softly weaving in his connexions, where Ibsen files his writing to a sharp point, and once the point has been made explicitly, it no longer holds the attention.   It was not the explicit statement at the end of the play—the "settlement of accounts"—which made Ibsen's writings appear so profoundly original to his generation, but the way in which it was induced.   He was like all great artists, at the growing point of his generation not in theory but in consciousness.[1] Nora's final proclaiming of the crusade was commonplace doctrine :   but the doctrine is embedded in a particular situation.   The theory had been "lived through".

Poor Nora, living by playing her tricks like a little pet animal, sensing how to manage Torvald by those pettinesses in his character she does not know she knows of, is too vulnerably sympathetic to find her life-work in reading John Stuart Mill.   At the end she still does not understand the strange world in which she has done wrong by forging a signature.   She does understand that she has lived by what Virginia Woolf called " the slow waterlogged sinking of her will into his ".   And this picture is built up for her and for us by the power of structural implication, a form of writing

[1] Ibsen himself recognized this (*Corr.*, pp. 214–5).   See below, ch. 4, p. 102.

particularly suited to drama, where the latent possibilities of
a long stretch of past time can be thrown into relief by a
crisis. In *A Doll's House*, the past is not only lighted up by
the present, as a transparency might be lit up with a lamp ;
the past is changed by the present so that it becomes a different
thing. Nora's marriage becomes eight years' prostitution, as
she gradually learns the true nature of her relations with
Torvald, and the true nature of Torvald's feelings for her.

In Act I, no less than six different episodes bring out the war
that is secretly waged between his masculine dictatorship
and her feminine wiles :

Her wheedling him for money with a simple transference :
" Let us do as *you* suggest. . . ."

Her promise to Christine : " Just leave it to me : I will
broach the matter very cleverly." She is evidently habituated
to, and aware of her own technique.

Her description of how she tried to coax Torvald into
taking the holiday and how she was saving up the story of the
bond " for when I am no longer as good-looking as I am now ".
She knows the precarious nature of her hold.

Her method of asking work for Christine by putting Christine also into a (completely bogus) position of worshipping
subservience to Torvald.

Her boast to Krogstad about her influence. Whilst this may
be a justifiable triumph over her tormentor, it is an unconscious
betrayal of Torvald (witness his fury in Act II at the idea of
being thought uxorious).

After this faceted exposition, the treatment grows much
broader. Nora admits Torvald's jealousy : yet she flirts with
Rank, aware but not acknowledging the grounds of her
control. The pressure of implication remains constant
throughout : it is comparable with the effect of a dialect,
colouring all that is said. To take a few lines at random from
the dialogue of Nora and Rank in Act II :

Nora (putting her hand on his shoulder) : Dear, dear Dr. Rank !
Death mustn't take you away from Torvald and me. [Nora
is getting demonstrative as she senses Rank's responsiveness,

G

and her hopes of obtaining a loan from him rise.   Hence her
warmth of feeling, purely seductive.]
Rank : It is a loss you will easily recover from.   Those who are
gone away are soon forgotten.   [Poor Rank is reminded by
that " Torvald and me " how little he really counts to Nora.]
Nora (anxiously) : Do you believe that ?   [Rank has awakened
her thoughts of what may happen if *she* has to go away.]

Her methods grow more desperate—the open appeal to
Torvald to keep Krogstad and the frantic expedient of the
tarantella.   In the last act her fate is upon her ; yet in spite
of all her terror, and Torvald's tipsy amorousness, she still
believes in his chivalry and devotion.   This extraordinary
self-deception is perhaps the subtlest and most telling implication of all.   Practice had left her theory unshaken : so when
the crash comes, she cries, " I have been living with a strange
man ", yet it was but the kind of man her actions had always
implied him to be. [Her vanity had completely prevented
her from recognizing what she was doing, even though she
had become such an expert at doing it.
Torvald is more gradually revealed.   In the first act he
appears indulgent, perhaps a trifle inclined to nag about the
macaroons and to preach, but virtually a more efficient David
Copperfield curbing a rather better-trained Dora.   In the
second act, his resentment and his pleasure alike uncover the
deeper bases of his dominance.   His anger at the prospect of
being thought under his wife's influence, and his fury at the
imputation of narrow-mindedness show that it is really based
on his own cowardice, the need for something weaker to bully :
this is confirmed when he gloats over Nora's panic as evidence
of her love for him, and over her agitation in the tarantella
(" you little helpless thing ! ").   His love of order and his
fastidiousness, when joined to such qualities, betray a set
personality ; and the last act shows that he has neither control
nor sympathy on the physical level.   But he is no fool, and
his integrity is not all cowardice.   Doubtless, debt or forgery
really was abhorrent to him.
The climax of the play comes when Nora sees Torvald and

sees herself : it is an *anagnorisis*, a recognition. Her life is cored like an apple. For she has had no life apart from this. Behind the irrelevant programme for self-education there stands a woman, pitifully inexperienced, numbed by emotional shock, but with a new-found will to face what has happened, to accept her bankruptcy, as, in a very different way, Peer Gynt had at last accepted his.

" Yes, I am beginning to understand. . . ." she says. " What you did," observes the now magnanimous Torvald, " you did out of love for me." " That is true," says Nora : and she calls him to a " settling of accounts ", not in any spirit of hostility but in an attempt to organize vacancy. " I have made nothing of my life. . . . I must stand quite alone . . . it is necessary to me . . ." That is really the programme. *Ainsi tout leur a craqué dans les mains*.[1]

The spare and laminated speech gains its effect by inference and riddle. But these are the characteristic virtues of Norse. Irony is its natural weapon. Ibsen was working with the grain of the language. It was no accident that it fell to a Norwegian to take that most finely tooled art, the drama, and bring it to a point and precision so nice that literally not a phrase is without its direct contribution to the structure. The unrelenting cohesion of *A Doll's House* is perhaps, like that of the *Œdipus the King*, too hard on the playgoer ; he is allowed no relief. Nora cannot coo to her baby without saying : " My sweet little *baby doll*! " or play with her children without choosing, significantly, *Hide and Seek*. Ibsen will not allow the smallest action to escape from the psychopathology of everyday life. However, a play cannot be acted so that every moment is tense with significance, and, in practice, an actor, for the sake of light and shade, will probably slur some of Ibsen's points, deliberately or unconsciously.[2] The tension

---

[1] Granville Barker, writing of *Cymbeline*, said that in the scene where Pisanio reveals Posthumus' instruction to murder her, the few brief words given to the Princess should show " an Imogen white from the fire ". This is equally true of Nora in Act III.

[2] James Agate complained that a producer slurred the effect of Rank's four last glowing words of thanks to Nora—" Thanks for the light "—by making Helmer give the light for his cigar, so that the words become

between the characters is such that the slightest movement of one sets all the others quivering. But this is partly because they are seen with such detachment, like a clear-cut intaglio. The play is, above all, articulated.

That is not to say that it is the mere dissection of a problem. Perhaps Rank and Mrs. Linde would have been more subtly wrought into the action at a later date ; but the tight control kept over Nora and Torvald does not mean that they can be exhausted by analysis or staled by custom. They are so far in advance of the characters of *Pillars of Society* that they are capable of the surprising yet inevitable development that marks the character conceived " in the round ", the character that is, in Ibsen's phrase, fully " seen ".

Consider, for example, Torvald's soliloquy whilst Nora is taking off her masquerade dress. It recalls at one moment Dickens's most unctuous hypocrites—" Here I will protect you like a hunted dove that I have saved from the claws of the hawk ! "—at another Meredith's Willoughby Patterne— " Only be frank and open with me and I will be both will and conscience to you "—yet from broadest caricature to sharpest analysis, it remains the self-glorified strut of the one character, the bank clerk in his pride, cousin to Peer Gynt, that typical Norwegian, and to Hjalmer Ekdal, the toiling breadwinner of the studio.

Whilst the Ibsenites might have conceded that Torvald is Art, they would probably have contended that Nora is Truth. Nora, however, is much more than a Revolting Wife. She is not a sour misanthropist or a fighting suffragette, but a lovely young woman who knows that she still holds her husband firmly infatuated after eight years of marriage. Hilda Wangel is another lovely young woman who can play Kitty O'Shea with no compunction. Rebekke, Thea, Asta are not of the tribe of Miss Buss and Miss Beale ; [1] and for each of them, the

---

meaningless. There are too many such points for any production to make them all—although it seems hard to deny Rank a strong exit.

[1] *Miss Buss and Miss Beale*
Cupid's darts do not feel.
How different from us
Are Miss Beale and Miss Buss.

hero would fling prudence to the winds and run exulting on
his ruin.

⌐In leaving her husband Nora is seeking a fuller life as a
human being. She is emancipating herself. Yet the seeking
itself is also a renunciation, a kind of death—" I must stand
alone.'⌐ No less than Falk, or the hero of *On the Vidda*, she
gives up something that has been her whole life. She is as
broken as Torvald in the end : but she is a strong character
and he is a weak one. In the " happy ending " which Ibsen
reluctantly allowed to be used, it was the sight of the children
that persuaded her to stay, and unless it is remembered that
leaving Torvald means leaving the children, the full measure
of Nora's decision cannot be taken. An actress gets her chance
to make this point in the reply to Torvald's plea that Nora
should stay for the children's sake.

It should be remembered, too, that the seriousness of the
step she takes is lost on the present generation. She was
putting herself outside society, inviting insult, destitution and
loneliness. She went out into a very dark night.[1]

Cause and effect do not work neatly in art. Many years'
hard work were behind the play where at last Ibsen's inheritance
ran into the fitting mould. Even the first versions of the play
were quite without the ironic implication which make it what
it is, although from the point of view of Ibsen the great moral
teacher there is little to choose between the first and final
versions. The irony may be too close-packed for stage
presentation, for Ibsen was always inclined to overdo things,
and as he had crowded the stage with characters in *Pillars of
Society*, so here he loads, and perhaps overloads, every rift
with ore. In Ibsen's great triumph in the ironic style, *Hedda
Gabler*, which appeared some ten years later and completed
the cycle that *A Doll's House* had begun, the variety of attack,
the different angles of approach, the way in which one position
after another is successively reversed or rejected, produce a

---

[1] When Thea runs away from her husband (in *Hedda Gabler*) the seriousness
of the situation is suggested by her begging Hedda to be *allowed* to call again ;
and by Hedda's reception of the news. " And you really had courage enough
for that ! "

final complexity far greater than that of *A Doll's House*, and yet the actor or producer is not faced with an *embarras de richesse* from which he is bound to select. Nevertheless, *A Doll's House* and *Hedda Gabler* are the same kind of play fundamentally : the likenesses count more than the differences.

The success of *A Doll's House* is a writer's success, and it depends on Ibsen's use of a personal prose style which was a natural development of the possibilities of his own language. Shakespeare occupies the place he does because he did better than anybody else the kind of thing the English language was particularly fitted to do, and at that period when it was sufficiently developed and yet sufficiently fluid to give the greatest freedom to experiment. It was rapidly expanding, but it had been worked into some degree of plasticity by Shakespeare's immediate predecessors. The splendid efflorescence of the comedies and of *Romeo and Juliet* follows hard on a period when Shakespeare was himself taking a spade and breaking up the soil—the period of the early histories, of *Henry VI* and *King John*. So excited were his contemporaries by these works that they seem for ever after to have remembered Shakespeare chiefly as the fashionable writer of sonnets, pathetic love scenes and high-class bawdry ; and this, like the popularity of Falstaff a little later, may have been supposed to have endured rather too persistently for the author's comfort.

Ibsen was in a position very similar to that in which Shakespeare found himself. In one lifetime immense strides could be made—the language was plastic, malleable, and comparatively unworked and unexhausted. But the virtues of Norse differ from the virtues of English. Instead of the scented, coloured opulence of the multifoliate rose, it has the austere, unchanging tenacity of the mountain pine. Instead of the play of metaphor, it offers riddling understatement, or ironic implication. This " bare, sheer, penetrating power " was above all characteristic of Ibsen. As Hopkins said of Dryden, he laid the strongest stress on the naked thew and sinew of the language. And this in a language which has no superfluous flesh.

No one else has ever written in Norse with quite the concentration attained by Ibsen. His poetry was concentrated, but for that very reason he succeeded best in the short lyric. Poetry was not a medium in which he found it possible to combine concentration and length. So he turned to prose. In *A Doll's House* his prose came to life. There had been individual flashes in the earlier plays—the whole part of Stensgård is a triumph of writing—but here for the first time it is not individuals, it is not incidents, but the homogeneity of the whole play which is achieved through the power of the word.

To his contemporaries, *A Doll's House* was a great work because it dealt powerfully and realistically with questions of personal importance to the spectators. Today, it survives as an impressive if limited work, based on a " problem of human nature in general," as Ibsen put it, and survives because it offers a particular artist's vision which is inseparable from the manner of its formulation. For Ibsen himself, it was a solution of the writer's problem of his medium, and heralded a new development of his work.

5

Ghosts, which appeared two years later, seemed to Ibsen's contemporaries even more the work of the great moral teacher, or even more shockingly improper, according to their views. Brieux's *Damaged Goods*, Hauptmann's *Before Sunrise*, and other modern moralities derive from such a reading. But sixty-three years after the scandal, the battle-cries and the tradition, *Ghosts* is more than a " documentary ". To begin with, it is not at all realistic. The inexorable chain of cause and effect is far too rationally exact for that. In real life, things don't work out so neatly. Osvald cannot run out without his hat but it portends something—that he will catch a chill and bring on his fit. The dice are loaded, as they are loaded in *Jude the Obscure* or *A Shropshire Lad*. The absence of God seems to involve a necessary malignancy in the

[1] Shaw, *Quintessence of Ibsenism*, p. 137.

" neutral " and vacant universe. *Ghosts* is not a tragedy but a nightmare, with the heightened repetition and re-echoing of a dream, the ingenious logical dovetailing of schizophrenia. It is of the world of Edgar Allen Poe and Hawthorn, rather than of Shaw and Brieux, and it depicts, with the meticulous organization of a logical mind on the verge of hysteria, the ultimate worst thing as it presented itself to Ibsen's generation ; poor puny humanity crushed between the upper and nether millstones of Society and Heredity. The pitiless judgment of the herd, as pronounced by Pastor Manders, balances the inexorable materialism of physiological inheritance. " All mankind has failed," said Ibsen at this time. He would not really have been comforted by the spectacle of Dr. Temple discussing the forbidden subject in the House of Lords, or by the advertisements of the Ministry of Health.

Ibsen had long been obsessed by this particular problem ; Dr. Rank, the murderer's children in *Brand*, Julian are all alike " sacrifices to Necessity ". Hereditary disease was for Ibsen the symbol of all the determinist forces that crush humanity down, as, in his poems, the figures of tortured animals had been the symbols of humanity's struggle. Here, he chose to set this particularly rigid form of determinism against the strongest of all the instincts. Unfortunately, the maternal passion is not a subject for drama. The Greeks and Shakespeare drew only unnatural mothers.[1] Mother-love is too simple and inflexible for the basis of drama ; because it is so unwavering, it ceases to be dramatically interesting. In *Peer Gynt* Åse's rôle is blended into Solveig's, where in the final scene Peer cries " My mother ! my wife ! " and Solveig sings over him the song of a mother to her child. She is the mother of the real Peer : she nourishes the seed of God. But in *Ghosts*, the maternal instinct is no more than an instinct ; it works efficiently but blindly. Ibsen's object in setting this force against the pitiless disease was simply to produce the strongest possible situation. The play is mechanically perfect in its logic, and the *peripeteia* are still exciting—particularly he revelation of Alving's life in Act I, and the last confessiont

[1] Except Constance in *King John*, and Hecuba in *The Trojan Women*.

of Osvald. But " all mankind has failed ". Every character is self-centred, from Regina to Mrs. Alving—who never attempted to see life from her husband's point of view, and only at the last moment sees it from her son's.

The old interpretation was that Mrs. Alving ought to have run away from her husband and that she illustrated what happened to Noras who did not run hard enough or far enough. But Ibsen would never have troubled to write a simple converse of a previous play. Mrs. Alving recognizes that she has helped to create the impossible situation by failing to understand Alving's gaiety and high spirits, and making his life miserable. Mrs. Alving's failure to realize how her husband was stifled by his surroundings is really a strong point against her, but the deadening effect of life " up the fjord " is perhaps taken too much for granted to be perceptible to an outsider. The longing to get away is known to nearly every Norwegian even today ; it may be transitory but it cannot be escaped. The sense of being shut in—shut in physically by the rainy fjord, shut in mentally by the small community— is given by the setting and by the use of Pastor Manders. Osvald's feelings on the subject are the same as his father's, and reflect what Ibsen himself had said of his own feelings in his letters.[1]

There is but one positive affirmation in the play, the speech in which Osvald describes *livsglaeden*, gladness of living, " the roll, the rise, the carol, the creation ". It is for him, as an artist, inseparable from *arbeitsglaeden*, the gladness of creation, or from his love for the " superbly healthy " body of Regina. But, Osvald adds :

I am afraid that all these feelings that are so strong in me would degenerate into something ugly here. . . . Even if one lived the same life here as over there, it would never really be the same life.

Ibsen is using the Norway from which he fled as symbol for all the limitations of life. Osvald's Paris is unreal : only the rain and the fjord exist. The happy lovers are unreal,

[1] See above, ch. 1, p. 7, note 4.

too. The world consists of Alving marriages and Engstrand Homes.

In her great speech of exposition, the *raisonneur's* speech of the play, Mrs. Alving uses an idea which Ibsen had expressed before, the idea of the rule of the past, the rule of ghosts.[1] In this play his own past, the ghost of his life in Norway, rules Ibsen. He had tried writing about subjects which had nothing to do with his own past, he had tried philosophic drama, he had repudiated nationalism, he had given up Christianity. The emptiness of his life was borne in on him. He, too, felt haunted by the spectres of the beliefs he thought he had cast out. There are two interpretations of this great speech : the contemporary interpretation—which was perhaps that of Ibsen himself—which would make it a rationalist's plea against all forms of belief that are not based on logic ; and the interpretation which would make it the cry of a divided mind. The ghosts are mighty. The darkness in which they live is a darkness in which all poets must walk. Had not Ibsen himself written a poem about his own powers as a writer being born of darkness, and fearing the light ?

> *Mrs. Alving :* Spectres. When I heard Osvald and Regina in there, it was as if I saw spectres before me. I'm nigh to believing we are spectres, the whole lot of us, Pastor Manders. It is not only that which we get from fathers and mothers, that moves about with us. There are all kinds of old extinct opinions, all kinds of old extinct creeds, and such-like things. They are not alive within us, but they stay with us all the same, and we can never be quit of them. I have only to take a paper and read it, and it's like seeing spectres stealing between the lines. There must be spectres all over the world. They must lie as thick as the sands, I feel. And we are so miserably, damnably light-fearing, the whole lot of us.

The matter may be that of the emancipated rationalist, but

[1] The phrase is no more than a metaphor for the foreigner, but for the Norwegian, moving in a countryside filled with legend, a community dominated by family traditions, the presence of the ghostly past and the rule of the dead were vivid and continuous experience, as can be seen also in *Rosmersholm* and *Bygmester Solness.*

the tone and the undertone is that of the haunted man, facing the Bøjg in the Northern mists. "Life is the troll" as Ibsen says in the poem (*Fear of Light*). Such horror is not logical : it is based on revulsion from the inhuman mechanism of existence. Against the darkness and the trolls is set Osvald's vision of the sun ; and it is remarkable that Norway's greatest painter, Edvard Munch, saw in the sun, as Osvald the painter did, the symbol of all that was divine within a dark and malignant world.[1]

The interest of *Ghosts* is historical. It exposes the materialist's nightmare, the price to be paid for a faith in the all-sufficiency of science, and the unreasonableness of rationalism. In fact, whether Mrs. Alving does or does not kill Osvald matters nothing to him, since he had ceased to exist as a human being. Ibsen is under a pseudo-scientific spell which allows us to look unblurred on suffering which is not known consciously at all. He omits from his calculation the fact that pain is an anæsthetic. But the rationalist's nightmare was the inspiration of his whole generation, from the shockers about invasions from Mars to the prognostics of the political economist. The natural pushed to such lengths acquires all the horrors of the supernatural in the mere fact that the universe produces syphilis, that society contrives to hush it up, and that the church is the biggest hypocrite of all. Ibsen would not seek refuge with the hedonism of Omar Khayyám. He would neither give nor take forgiveness for the state of the universe. In fact—unlike Carlyle's young friend—he would not even accept it. He felt that all mankind had failed.

Put out the light—and then, put out the light.

[1] In 1883, two years after *Ghosts* appeared, Munch paid his first visit to Paris. He was painting pictures like *A Sick Girl*, in which a young girl sits in a chair with her face turned to the sun, or *The Next Day*, a prostitute asleep on a bed. In an article in *The Norseman* for November 1943, Rolf Stenersen says that for Munch : "The sun was the origin of all things, but it did not interfere with the affairs of men. Men were the lice of the earth who loved and suffered : pawns in a game, whose purpose was apparently only to keep alive. . . . All went on. The sun was the primary source of energy and light."

Munch's greatest work, *The Frieze of Life*, is a series of symbolic pictures on a scale to recall the great sculpture of Rubek in *When we Dead Wake*.

6

The result was a miraculous clearing of the air. The storm
raised by *Ghosts* was far more violent than any of the other
storms which Ibsen had raised ; but this time he found that
he enjoyed it. He had friends and a party ; most of the battles
took place on paper, and on paper Ibsen would not only hold
his ground, but was prepared to counter-attack. Insults were
screamed and abuse was hurled at him, but in a year he turned
out *An Enemy of the People*, a fighting reply of the liveliest
kind. It is characteristic that this reply did not take the form
of polemics but of a play. Ibsen felt he had no existence
apart from his art. Dr. Stockmann is not a self-portrait.
" The Doctor and I get on very well together," wrote Ibsen
to his publisher, " we agree on so many subjects. But the
Doctor is a more muddle-headed person than I am." [1]

The Doctor is not intellectually very subtle, it is true. He
makes his stand for honesty partly on instinct (as Falstaff " on
instinct " is a coward) and partly out of obstinacy and a wild
love for a fight. His irrepressible high spirits, his absurd
optimism, his utter disregard for his own or his family's
position, or even the future of his best pair of trousers are
far removed from his acutely self-conscious and self-controlled
creator. As the mob break Stockmann's windows, he runs
about in his dressing-gown, picking up the stones, and crying
with enthusiasm : " I shall treasure these stones as relics."
It is pretty certain that in like circumstances Ibsen would have
crawled under the table. But on the other hand, Ibsen would
not have expected his discovery about the bath water to have
been received with rejoicing.[2]

Stockmann is a truly Norwegian figure. He has quite a
lot in common with Peer Gynt, something, too, with Dr.

[1] *Corr.*, p. 359.

[2] Ibsen used the symbol of the bath water elsewhere to describe the difference
between himself and Zola. I descend into the mud to wash myself, he observed, but Zola descends to wallow.

Wangel and Engineer Borgheim. The little town, with its local politics, and its towns-meetings, its magnates and its public benefactors, is clearly the same sort of little town as that shown in *Pillars of Society* and *The League of Youth*. But though Ibsen and the Doctor are in earnest in attacking the problems of the *lokale forholde* they can also laugh at them. The true spirit of comedy lies in not being obsessed and helpless in the face of upheavals and discomforts. Stockmann revived the gusto of Falk in *Love's Comedy*, and could find exhilaration in a riot, and encouragement in a boycott.

It was long since Ibsen had written anything so full of verve ; the most audacious aspect of the play is its note of confidence. As a result of the attacks upon him, Ibsen was confirmed that he was indeed an artist, and that ten years later the majority would accept his views, whilst he would have moved farther on.[1] And so he did. Adherents of the doctrine of Progress might have found material in the story of his career. The highest proof of his greatness is that never, to the end of his life, did he show any tendency to grow fixed and set either in his views or his methods. The tendency is almost inevitable in those who begin as reformers. Opposition confirms them, so that the effort needed to maintain their position tends to harden them in it ; further advance is not possible ; and they are liable to end their lives as advocates of the *status quo*.

Such was not the case with Ibsen. He moved forward to a new and greater play—some would say, his greatest play— wherein he ruthlessly satirized his own devoted followers. The satire was, however, combined with a new depth and richness. It was as if the poet had revived in him. In two years' time, which was henceforth to be the regular interval between his plays, appeared *The Wild Duck*.

[1] " In ten years the majority will possibly occupy the standpoint which Dr. Stockmann held at the public meeting. But during these ten years the Doctor will not have been standing still. He will be at least ten years ahead of the majority. He can never have the majority with him. As regards myself, I am conscious of incessant progression. At the point where I stood when I wrote each of my books, there now stands a tolerably compact crowd : but I myself am no longer there : I am elsewhere : further ahead, I hope." (*Corr.*, p. 370.)

Chapter Four

THE HUMANIST

" The Wild Duck "—" The Sea Woman "
" Rosmersholm "—" Hedda Gabler "

IN the four plays which lie at the centre of his work, Ibsen
is no longer the State Satirist, no longer the man the Ibsenites
thought he was. In each of these plays, it is life—complex,
delicate, and vulnerable—which he sets against systems of
thought, however advanced and high-minded, and against
merely intellectual convictions, however sincere. The advocates of the New Morality were ten years behind Ibsen,
although they thought they had found their champion. But
Ibsen had ceased to be polemical ; the need for generosity
and selflessness could not be hammered home with the concentrated fierceness appropriate to advocating intellectual
honesty.

In these four plays, Ibsen is always for the complex as
against the simple solution, for the scrupulous as against
the doctrinaire mind. Gregers, Kroll and Tesman have
in common the great failing which was for Ibsen the sin
without forgiveness : too much of their mind works auto-
matically. Their opinions have hardened and ossified,
and cut them off from full experience of what happens to
them. The disease takes a subtler form in them than in
Helmer or Manders ; in Tesman it is only the pedant's short-
sightedness—which can entertain or even endear in the
absent-minded professor. Yet how completely he is damned !
the more completely because Ibsen allows him kindliness,
disinterested friendship and humility which Helmer and
Manders are denied. Ibsen's own intolerance and intellectual arrogance had mitigated. He no longer wanted to
torpedo the Ark.

That these plays should have been distorted into a Pro-

gramme of Reform is a final irony which could not have
been lost on Ibsen himself. He gave up trying to explain
them. He merely continued to write.

The subject of the plays is human relationships in the
fullest sense. Not the strong situation, the meeting of " the
fell incensèd point of mighty opposites ", but the half-sensed,
half-obliterated ties of ordinary life ; the trusts, the stabilities,
the adhesions of older, more settled modes of feeling. The
characters—quite naturally, quite inevitably—are getting
nearer to middle age. The method is becoming less theatrical, less explicit. The conscious discipline and control
which make *A Doll's House* and *Ghosts* such obvious models
for young writers—which evoked imitations such as Hauptmann's *Before Sunrise*—were replaced by a subtler and less
conscious discipline, a control which was more indirect but
more comprehensive. The last relics of the school of Scribe
were disappearing also.

Hedda's game with the pistols is a very different use of
conventional material from Nora's dancing of the tarantella.
The pistols are consciously theatrical to herself and to the
others, they are part of her " life-craving ". The melodrama
of the pistols is set against the background of Aunt Julle's
domesticities and Tesman's solicitudes, and the implications
are ironic. The four plays show indeed a progressive severity
of control, until in *Hedda Gabler* the screw is turned so tightly
that Ibsen has achieved the perfect specimen piece. Like *A
Doll's House*, *Hedda Gabler* is so finished a production that it
brought Ibsen himself to a full stop, and he began again in a
new way, whilst his disciples found it a model upon which
they could base their own variations.

There is no answer to Hedda. Even the Ibsenites could not
find a problem in this play.[1] But equally there is no answer
to Rebekke or Rosmer, to Hjalmer, Gregers and Hedvig,
and the answer to Ellida does not meet the deepest implications of her need. In an age which was always certain, even
if it were only certain that no certainty existed, an age which

[1] See the preface to Archer's translation in the *Collected Works*, (Vol. X,
p. xvii).

was Rationalist in its scepticism and Positivist in its doubt, Ibsen saw, and not dogmatically but deliberately set it down, that the method of question and answer, of problem and solution, is no method for the artist.

The Wild Duck and Rosmersholm are the ripest of Ibsen's plays. Peer Gynt and Bygmester Solness may range wider and probe deeper, but here are his most masterful and most harmonious works. Vision and craftsmanship, power and skill are in equilibrium. These were not plays to be imitated by the disciples, for they depend on qualities in the writing that belong only to Ibsen himself.

Like Hamlet, The Wild Duck can be interpreted by each man in his own image. "The single vision" deepened and grew mysteriously active, mutable and various; the tide rises and falls, the light fades and gleams; to seek definitions is to go and catch a falling star. One day it will read as a tragedy, the next as the harshest irony; parts of it are clumsy, in other parts are embedded old controversies of that time. So searching yet so delicate is the touch, that these flaws and vagaries seem in themselves to strengthen the work. In this play and in Rosmersholm Ibsen perfected his own special power; the power to infuse the particular, drab, limited fact with a halo and a glory.

A room is to him a room, a writing table a writing table, and a waste paper basket, a waste paper basket [says Mrs. Woolf]. At the same time, the paraphernalia of reality have at certain moments to become the veil through which we see infinity. When Ibsen achieves this, as he certainly does, it is not by performing some miraculous conjuring trick at the critical moment. He achieves it by putting us into the right mood from the very start and by giving us the right materials for his purpose. He gives us the effect of ordinary life . . . but he gives it us by choosing a very few facts and those of a highly relevant kind. Thus when the moment of illumination comes, we accept it implicitly. We are neither roused nor puzzled; we do not have to ask ourselves, What does this mean? We simply feel that the thing we are looking at is lit up, and its depths revealed. It has not ceased to be itself by becoming something else. . . . The object which has been so uncompromisingly solid becomes, or should become, luminously transparent.[1]

Mrs. Woolf is describing a poet's power ; it reads almost as a paraphrase of Wordsworth's aims in the preface to *Lyrical Ballads*. Ibsen had suppressed the poet in himself but this suppressed power lights up his writing, giving it not only the rich concentration of *A Doll's House*, but the unifying cohesion of the symbolic.

The rationalist students of Ibsen tried to pin a single meaning on to his symbols ; was the wild duck symbolic of Hedvig or of Hjalmer or of Gregers ? was Gregers a portrait of Ibsen or was he not ? No one is likely to react in that way now. The photographer's studio, that most oddly particular and specific scene, and the attic which is the refuge of the maimed, the solitary and the defeated, with dusty trees and stopped clocks, and fragments of half a dozen smashed lives—these are the ocean depths that reflect infinity.

> *The Mind, that Ocean where each kind*
> *Does streight its own resemblance find ;*
> *Yet it creates, transcending these,*
> *Far other Worlds and other Seas.*

The old lumber room was a childhood memory of Ibsen : he too had brooded over the old *History of London* " with the figures of Death and a girl", the old dumb German clock (" for time has stopped in there ") and the other treasures of long-dead sailors.

Everyone knows the fascination of lumber rooms : this one seems alive ; to old Ekdal it represents the great forests, to Hedvig the depths of the sea, but she also says : " Yes, it has many changes. In the morning it looks quite different from the evening, and in the rain very different from what it does in fine weather."

Outside are the tools of the photographer for making dead reproductions of life ; inside, wild life in captivity and stagnation (in Ibsen's own poem the wild duck represented the

---

[1] *The Death of the Moth* (Hogarth, 1942), p. 108.

H

poet). That Ibsen could use the setting in this way meant
that he had mastered the most intractable part of his equipment. The scene-painter and property manager who ruled
the stage of the day, and spoiled so many plays, had been
taken into the heart of the mystery. Aristotle said the
spectacle was the least important part of the tragedy ; and
for that reason it is the most dangerous. Even in earlier
plays, the scene and the atmosphere had played some part—
the warmth and festivity of the magic circle, the Christmas
tree and candles of *A Doll's House* are surrounded by the
tingling snow and the frozen fjord.

In *The Wild Duck* the attic lures the Ekdals as Little Eyolf
is charmed by the Rat Wife, or Ellida by the stranger whose
eyes change with the changing tides. They live in dreams,
and this is their dream country. There is death in such
dreaming—sudden collision with the world of pistols, of
scaffolding, of piers running out into the water, and Hedvig
or Eyolf is swept away.

Yet Hedvig cannot understand Greger's question " Are you
sure it's an attic ? " " Sure it's an attic ? " she echoes. And
there is plenty of evidence that it is an attic, the scene for
four out of five acts of an extremely well-made play. The
play begins slowly—the first act is all intrigue and ponderous
sociabilities, the second is almost pure comedy of the Ekdals
at home. In the third act, Gregers begins his reform of
Hjalmer and is himself mercilessly dissected by Relling, but
also has another scene with his father. Only in the last two
acts does the storm break.

The Norwegian background is not used for the plot, as in
Ghosts, but it pervades the play. The provincial society of
Act I, stuffy, complacent, and dictatorial, might belong to
other lands, though nowhere was its power greater than in
Norway. But the odd combination of Bohemianism and
photography, the quirks of Gregers and Ekdal and Molvik
could flourish only in Norwegian tolerance of eccentricity,
of crotchety independence. And the shut-in attic opens out
till it reveals " all the great Hoidal forest ", as, between the
houses of any Norwegian town, suddenly, beyond the chimney

pots, appear the towering peaks, or the high stretches of the
vidda.[1]

Ibsen was not drawing upon this and that memory of his
past, he was musing over the little towns of Skien and Grimstad, Hedvig his little sister, the old lumber room, his starved
and painful life on the fringes of "good society". As for
the language, it tastes of that common, rough, terse speech
which appeared with Engstrand in *Ghosts*.[2] Hjalmer spins
his clichés, Gina is apt but ungrammatical, Relling is curtly
simple.

> *Relling :* But while I think of it, Mr. Wehrle the younger, leave
> out that foreign word, ideals. We have a good Norse word :
> lies.

It is Gregers, however, who sums up the Wild Duck's story in
the lilting poetic line : " And so she has dwelt in the ocean
depths." (Og så har hun vaeret på havsens bund.)
Hedvig asks him why he doesn't call it " havets bund, eller
havbunden " but when he asks her why he shouldn't use the
poetic phrase she says, " It seems to me so strange, to hear
another person say 'The ocean depths'." And he presses
her until she admits that this is what she too has called the
attic to herself.

The piteous little phrase " It seems to me so strange "
reoccurs like a *leitmotif* in Hedvig's part. Her failing sight,
her childish attempts to understand what the grown-ups mean
by their behaviour, and the luring phantasies of her own
dreams are all reflected in it : " that sounds so strange to
me ", " I think that is so strange " (mig høres det så underligt : det her synes jeg er underligt). Hjalmer's unending
twaddle is pierced by her bare cries : " Ah, darling, darling
father ! " . . . " He's gone from us, mother ! He's gone
from us ! He'll never come back again ! " Greger's whole
life is governed by phrases and not by experience ; this is the

[1] In Bergen, for instance, the heights of Fløjen can be seen from the German
Quay or the Fishmarket.
[2] A. Ansternsen, *The Proverb in Ibsen* (Columbia, 1936), notes that Hjalmer,
Old Engstrand, and Peer Gynt are the greatest users of proverbs in Ibsen.

root of his disaster. When Hjalmer rushes out, he says to Gina : " Would it not be better, all the same, first to let him fight his bitter fight to the end ? " " Oh, he can do that afterwards," retorts Gina. " The first thing to do is to quiet the child." Gregers is something of a poet : the fatal point is, he is a bad poet.

The old view of *The Wild Duck* was that it presented the obverse case to *A Doll's House* and *Ghosts*, and gave a timely warning against fanatic innovators. In this view the centre of the play lies in the mistakes of Gregers and the diagnosis of Relling, the only two characters capable of judgment or of moral decision.) This is its " problem ". As Shaw puts it :

> Now an interesting play cannot in the nature of things mean anything but a play in which problems of conduct and character of personal importance to the audience are raised and suggestively discussed.[1]

Three times Gregers the idealist crosses swords with Relling the psychologist and the play ends with their mutual defiance. The structure depends on Greger's interventions ; he is responsible not only for the breach between Gina and Hjalmer but also for the suggestion which drives Hedvig to her death. It may be that Gregers was a more interesting figure to contemporaries than he is today ; but the fact is that although Gregers sets the play in motion, he is not the centre of interest. Ibsen himself seems to have shifted his ground as he wrote. We have indeed his own word that he did not think in terms of " problems ", " Everything which I have written as a poet has had its origin in a frame of mind and situation in life. I never wrote because I had, as they say, ' found a good subject ' ",[2] and in explanation of the artist's attitude to science : " What we, the uninitiated, do not possess as knowledge, we possess, I believe, to a certain degree, as intuition or instinct." He goes on to say that there is a kind of family likeness between scientists and artists of the same period, just as in portraits—he observes—there is a type characteristic of a given period, independent of any school of painters.[3]

[1] *Quintessence of Ibsenism*, p. 137   [2] *Corr.*, p. 198.   [3] *Corr.*, pp. 214–5.

Ibsen's own anticipation of psychological discoveries is itself a testimony to his theory ; the most striking instance is *The Sea Woman*.

Ibsen would therefore in any case have repudiated the idea that in *The Wild Duck* he was being merely instructive. But it does appear that he began with the notion of a satiric comedy, rather in the mood of *An Enemy of the People*. The first act is out of key with what follows, although it is an excellent sketch of provincial good society in all its smug solidarity—a society which has made catspaws of the weak, as Ibsen had already depicted. Wehrle the elder is another Consul Bernick. In this society Gregers is playing the part of social reformer, and, as in all literature of the time, from *Aurora Leigh* to *Beauchamp's Career*, the way of the social reformer is thorny indeed. On the other hand, the social reformer is conscious of the nobility of his vocation, and is thus enabled to withstand all the fiery darts of the wicked and to hurl a pretty dart in turn. Miss Aurora Leigh—a notable social reformer—bids Lady Waldemar remember how

You sold that poisonous porridge called your soul,

and, beside her invective, Gregers's words to old Wehrle sound almost filial.[1] But the force of these scenes is almost entirely lost upon the reader of today.

In a sense, of course, Gregers is a permanent figure ; he is the man who has found the entire solution to life in a creed, whether that of Marx or Freud, the Oxford Group or Yoga. He is Brand turned inside out. He sees his mother as right and his father as wrong. He feels wronged by his father, and at the same time morbidly conscious of a duty towards Hjalmer, so he is driven to interference. In none of his high-minded attempts does he pay any attention to the delicate human material he is handling—being what Hedda Gabler called "a specialist". Nevertheless, Relling's brutalities are beside the mark. Gregers himself is mentally abnormal and, as he hints, physically a doomed man.

The play begins with his story ; but the Ekdals run away

[1] *Aurora Leigh* was written by Mrs. Browning in 1857.

with it. Ibsen said in a letter to his publisher, " The characters of *The Wild Duck* have endeared themselves to me ",
and by the characters, he clearly meant the Ekdals. Relling
does his best to keep the play on a straight line with his sermon
on the life-fantasy—in which he was anticipated by Francis
Bacon ; [1] but in the later acts Gregers is chiefly a " feed " to
the Ekdals ; he knits up an episode, or evokes a confidence
from Hjalmer or Hedvig, but has little independent life.

The Ekdals gleam with vitality, even the sodden old
Lieutenant. They are complex people who have simple
minds. In the scene where old Ekdal decides to show Gregers
the wild duck, they infect one another with excitement, until
at last Hjalmer, who had begun by being rather ashamed of
his hobby, joins in the chorus.

> *Lieut. Ekdal :* That's where the rabbits go at night, old man !
> *Gregers :* No, really ? you've got rabbits too ?
> *Lieut. Ekdal :* Yes, you can well believe we've got rabbits. He's
> asking if we've got rabbits, Hjalmer ! Aha ! But now comes
> the great thing. look you ! Now for it ! Look out, Hedvig !
> Stand here : like that : now look in. Do you see a basket
> full of straw ?
> *Gregers :* Yes. And I see there's a bird in the basket.
> *Lieut. Ekdal :* Aha—" a bird " !
> *Gregers :* Isn't it a duck ?
> *Lieut. Ekdal :* Yes, you can bet it's a duck !
> *Hjalmer :* But WHAT SORT of duck, do you think ?
> *Hedvig :* It's not an ordinary duck——
> *Lieut. Ekdal :* Sh ! Sh !

In this second act, the charm and absurdity of the Ekdals
are enhanced by their innocent self-deceptions. The old man
pretending he wants his hot water only for his ink, Hjalmer
crying " No beer at a moment like this ! Give me my
flute ! " are safe in the hands of their womenfolk, practising

[1] " Doth any man doubt that if there were taken out of men's minds
vain opinions, flattering hopes, false valuations, imaginations as one would,
and the like, but it would leave the minds of a number of men poor shrunken
things, full of melancholy and indisposition, and unpleasing to themselves."
(*Essays :* Of Truth.)

the ancient conspiratorial art of "managing father". (What is humiliation for Nora becomes a game for Gina and Hedvig) It is a housecraft handed down from mother to daughter with the family recipes and ranging from maxims like "Feed the brute"—"Beer, father! lovely cool beer!" cries Hedvig— to that genuine faith in the Great Inventor which only the simple and childish could entertain, but which is the basis of Hjalmer's well-being. / For he is a timid soul, easily snubbed, and needs the constant worship of his family to keep him in good heart. Hence his fretfulness at any suggestion of criticism, he feels betrayed from within the citadel.

Unsparingly as he is exposed, Hjalmer is not condemned. He, too, had endeared himself to Ibsen. He is not a Pecksniff or even a Skimpole—rather is he a Micawber. When his preparation for heroic flight is punctured by Gina's "But what about all the rabbits?" he first cries despairingly, "What! have I got to take all the rabbits with me?" but almost at once wrests the alarming situation to his own advantage—"Father must get used to it. There are higher things than rabbits, which I have had to give up." His meanest act is when he gets Hedvig to finish his work so that he can potter in the attic, but salves his conscience by saying: "Don't hurt your eyes, do you hear? I'm not going to answer for it: you must decide for yourself, and so I warn you."

But his relish of the "patent contrivance" and his passionate concern about "a new path to the water-trough" are at least evidence of *livsglaeden* if not of *arbeitsglaeden*. He is so childish that he asks only for a part to play and an audience to applaud. Old Wehrle's cast-off mistress and her child are the perfect audience—docile, responsive, uncritical. His anger when he first suspects Hedvig not to be his is blind, savage and genuine.

Hjalmer : My home's in ruins! (Bursts into tears.) Gregers, I have no child now!
Hedvig : What's that? Father! Father!
Gina : Look at that, now!

Hjalmer : Don't come near me, Hedvig ! Go away . . . I can't bear to see her. Ah . . . her eyes . . . Goodbye.
Hedvig (screams) : No ! No ! Don't leave me !
Gina : Look at the child, Hjalmer ! Look at the child !
Hjalmer : I won't ! I can't ! I'm going—away from all this.

But his later cruelty is false play-acting. " In these last minutes in my old home I wish to be free from—intruders ! " " Does he mean me, mother ? " asks Hedvig, trembling. In his last explanation to Gregers, Hjalmer admits his dependence on her love and hero-worship, a little too clearly to be completely in character. " There is that terrible doubt—perhaps Hedvig never really loved me . . ." and he makes up a fantasy of how Hedvig had all the time been really laughing at him and deceiving him.[1] The appetite for proof of affection is begotten of anxiety, and in this confession, Hjalmer becomes pitiable, because he, too, is seen to be bankrupt, and broken. Selfish and parasitic as his love was, it sprang from and satisfied his deepest need.

Hjalmer is both a tragic and a comic figure : Hedvig, like Antigone and Cordelia, is the victim who redeems. She is a mere child, saying prayers for the wild duck " that it may be preserved from all harm ", and making her deep-laid plans to keep father in good humour. But she is mysterious too : like the wild duck, no one knows " where she came from, or who her friends are "—it is essentially an open question whether she is Hjalmer's child or old Wehrle's ; and she is subject to strange adolescent tides of feeling that rise " from the ocean depths ". Hedvig's piteous limitations leave her exposed to catastrophe. She does believe in Hjalmer, as no one but a child could do. He is her God and when he betrays her, she is terror-stricken with all the final black despair of childhood. Gregers, in prompting her to kill the wild duck, uses the language of religion. It is to be a witness-bearing, a ritual sacrifice, to propitiate Hjalmer, the offended God.

[1] This is curiously enough the main theme of Helge Krog's play, *On Life's Sunny Side*, which was produced in 1944 by the Arts Theatre in London. The husband's testing of his wife is very reminiscent of Gregers's test for Hedvig.

And so when Hjalmer presents his final " demand of the ideal "
—" If I were to say, 'Hedvig, art willing to give up this *life*
for me ?'—thanks, you'd soon see the answer ! '" Hedvig
puts the pistol to her own breast and fires.   Yet it is unresolved
whether she died in grief or as a sacrifice ; from an adolescent
impulse to self-destruction, or a childish desire for revenge—
" I'll die and *then* you'll be sorry."

Her death is catastrophic, the only unambiguous event in
the play ; yet its causes are veiled.   It is not related to the
previous action by the kind of iron chain that draws on
Osvald's death.   It is a shock yet inevitable.   Gina, gathering
the remnants of her poor tenderness, speaks the last word :
" The child mustn't lie out here to be looked at.   She shall
go in her own little room, my pet."

The most mysterious and potent symbol of all is not a
human character but the wild duck itself.   Each of the characters
has something in common with the wild duck's story, but
that story reflects all the scattered lights of the play and focuses
them in one.   The potency and power of the wild duck is
that of the ghost in *Hamlet*, or the witches in *Macbeth* : it
unites and concentrates the implications which lie behind the
action of individuals.

Relling's final gibe at Gregers belongs to another world—
the world of judgments, views and reason ; the greatness of
this play is that it moves upon so many levels simultaneously.
Ibsen was no longer limited by his chosen technique.   The
freedom and scope of *The Wild Duck* are a symptom of that
increasing depth of humanity and generosity which was
taking Ibsen further and further from the doctrinal and the
propagandist.   " Dramatic categories ", he observed, " are
elastic and must accommodate themselves to literary fact."
The characters had endeared themselves to him and the
dramatic category was modified accordingly, so that even
the weakest is allowed to hint that he too has known " the
ocean's depths ".

2

When he finished *The Wild Duck*, Ibsen began work on
The Sea Woman, and although it was not finished till after
Rosmersholm, the links with *The Wild Duck* remain closest.
This is a play which has improved with the years.   It was
not very popular when it was written, but on its revival in
1928, it seemed like a contemporary work on the latest psychological principles.[1]   The exorcism of Ellida's obsession by
giving her freedom of choice is perhaps new psychology, but
it is very old drama.   It is the way Volumnia wins Coriolanus :

> *Come, let us go :*
> *This fellow had a Volscian to his mother :*
> *His wife is in Corioli, and his child*
> *Like him by chance.*

But *The Sea Woman* fails, because in spite of the dramatic
story, it lacks that final unity which should fuse the poetry
and mystery and terror of the ocean depths which lure Ellida
with their vehicle—the problems of small-town life, and the
ennui of the unemployed wife, which is also the problem of
Hedda Gabler and Rita Allmers.   The minor figures are
somewhat clumsily fitted in—the two girls who began as the
daughters of Rosmer but were worked into this play, and
one of whom, the " wicked " Hilde, was to reappear later as
the " bird of prey ".   Here, a malicious child with a secret
passion for her stepmother, she is touched in rather too sharply
and brilliantly for the opalescent and shifting interplay of the
main theme.   Bolette, who marries mediocrity to get a place
in the world, is too clearly a foil for Ellida : Ellida herself, the
mermaid, ought to be enchanting, but we are so obviously
told what to feel about her that we do not feel it.

The scene however—surely it is Moldefjord, which Ibsen
visited in 1885 [2]—is masterly done.   The last visit of the

---

[1] It has recently been revived at the Chanticleer and Arts Theatres (1945)
in London, and the Gate Theatre in Dublin.

[2] Koht agrees (II, p. 246).

steamer before winter—the walk upon the hillside to the little
park and The Pilot's View where the band plays on Sundays—
the little town dominating the islands and the lighthouse down
at Sandvik—the flag hoisted for a birthday—in all this there
is the very breath of the west coast, the prim amenities and
rural dignities surrounded by the steepness of the fjells, and
the wash of the tides, and the salt smell of the bladderwrack
blowing up from the shore.   And the stranger who weds
Ellida to himself and to the sea, whose eyes change with the
changing of the tides—his power over Ellida may be exorcized
by Wangel, but it is as if Catherine Earnshaw had turned
from the moors and Heathcliff to the comfort of Thrush-
cross Grange.[1]   Prudence, wisdom, and sanity are on Wangel's
side, yet the Stranger is an emissary from the hidden sources
of power, and there is a contradiction at the basis of the play.
The poetic vision, which should control and focus all the
dramatic action is, instead, set in opposition to it.   Conse-
quently, in spite of the beauty and power of individual scenes,
the play betrays a certain lack of proportion.

3

Rosmersholm, on the contrary, is Ibsen's most perfectly
balanced work.   Architecturally, he never produced anything so harmonious : it is his most Sophoclean play.   He
was himself on the verge of a great reconciliation.   After the
visit to Norway in 1885—the first for eleven years—he produced three intensely Norwegian plays—*Rosmersholm, The
Sea Woman* and *Hedda Gabler*—and then, in 1891, at the age
of sixty-three, he returned home for good.   With characteristic perversity, he invented all sorts of excuses—that it was
easier to deal with questions of copyright and property in a
country where he had full citizenship : that he wanted to
be near his son, now a rising civil servant, and married to

[1] The Stranger is a challenger and a judge—like the Strange Hunter of
On the Vidda, the Button Moulder, and the Rat Wife.

Bjørnson's daughter : that he needed to settle down. But
Ibsen had never been used to put either money or family ties
before his work. He was no longer the wounded wild duck,
flying south to the coasts of the sun ; he was turning again
to his own people and knitting up his life with theirs.

Rosmersholm is the most clearly located of all the plays ;
the old manor house at Molde can be identified as the scene.
Rebekke comes from Finmark, in farthest northern Norway,
that desolate region of the polar night and the midnight sun.[1]

Rosmer and Rebekke are figures of heroic magnitude set
in a scene isolated and haunted. The feeling of remoteness,
of all other life being far distant, the silence and circumscribed
self-sufficiency of the homestead belongs to Norway, a land
of great distances and far-scattered dwellings. Life at Rosmersholm is cut off from life elsewhere, and in this isolation the
rule of the dead is strengthened. The power of the dead
Rosmers, the sense of their presence and of the presence of the
dead wife, springs from that Norse inheritance of the supernatural which Ibsen had already drawn on in *Brand*, *Peer
Gynt*, and *Ghosts*. Here it is not the trolls of the mountains
but the spirits of the homestead which haunt the minds of the
living. The sense of a ghostly world impinging on humanity
has persisted in Norse literature from the time of the Eddas
to the latest poems of the day—Nordahl Grieg wrote of the
war dead as " ghosts looming through minds of new men ".[2]

Such a spiritual climate breeds heroic character but breeds
it for a tragic destiny. The primitive horror of the old house-
keeper—

> *No help here ! the dead wife has taken them*

sums up, in the last line of the play, all the living force of these
dark powers.

In lesser ways the play is dependent on the particular

[1] She describes the passion that swept over her as like one of the storms
that sweep the northern seas ; and the peace of her love for Rosmer as like
the silence of the bird-cliffs under the midnight sun. Rebekke is essentially
of North Norway. Ellida's Stranger also came from Finmark.

[2] " De spøker i nye menn " (" De Beste ", *Friheten*). (Helgafell. Reyk-
javik, 1944.)

problems of Norwegian life. Rosmer, like Brand, finds himself embroiled in the political difficulties that result from the impact of the national situation upon local politics. The political crisis which rends the local parties and the family of Rektor Kroll was based on the contemporary struggle of the King and the Ministers to override the Storthing (the legislative body), which was more radical than the Executive. But the qualities of the play do not depend on these accidentals of time and space, although it gains from having such particular roots, no doubt. There is a penetrating veracity which recalls George Eliot ; yet, held in this lucid depth, is a vision which is no part of the story, though reflected in it, where

forever
It trembles yet it cannot pass away.

The organization is superb. All Ibsen's technical achievements since *A Doll's House* are summed up in this play. The use of implication, including what came to be called his " retrospective method " ; scenic suggestion ; the forging of a chain of tiny events to give scale to the great crises. Some of the earlier drafts contain what appear in the light of the finished play to be fantastic details—in one, Rebekke is Rosmer's wife, in another she is governess to his two daughters ; and from the shock of these incongruities can be estimated the justness of the " selected events ".

The play has an exact symmetry : the first half deals with Rosmer, and the second with Rebekke : Act I with his present, Act II with his past, Act III with Rebekke's past and Act IV with her present. But the story of the two is one story, as they recognize at the end. " Man and wife shall go together . . . for now we two are one."

They accept their guilt ; being adult, they recognize it. It is the first time since *Brand* and *Peer Gynt* that Ibsen had admitted the idea of personal guilt, personal responsibility. A murderess, an apostate priest, a suicide pact, incest in the background—the amount of sheer horror in this play doubles and trebles that in any of his previous plays. Yet there is no sense of bewilderment, horror or injustice, because the positive qualities of Rebekke and Rosmer—her courage and his kindness—are never found wanting.

In Rosmer, the good as well as the bad side of heredity is stressed. His conversion to freethinking is froth upon the surface of his character. Whatever his views, he does not live by bread alone. The traditions of his race have bred in him a fineness of purpose, a capacity for the inner life which he can no more escape than he can escape the characteristic traits of melancholy. Though Rosmer has lost his beliefs, he has retained all the scruples and the standards which these beliefs indoctrinated, and has grafted them on to Rebekke. They each modify the other—she moulding his intellect, he transforming her impulses. In the first act, we see him attempting to strike for freedom ; but Mortensgård disillusions him, and awakens his conscience about Beate. The political nastiness of Mortensgård with his nice calculation of how much enlightenment is expedient, is as foreign to Rosmer as the bigoted rage of Kroll. But Rosmer's dreams of a "chivalry of the common people" are not political at all— they are ethical. And his disillusionment in his own power to create this chivalry springs from his recognition of the deadly fact, which Kroll emphasizes in Act I : "You are so terribly impressionable." [1] Rebekke has moulded him—he recognizes it. She had planned his conversion, she had planned to use him. He feels himself utterly uprooted when she, who had given him this new life, seems to have betrayed him. He himself thinks of suicide before Ulric Brendel, his old tutor, puts the last suggestion into his mind—the craving for a test which will give him a firm foothold in this horrible welter of instability. His testing of Rebekke is like her tempting of Beate, an insidious temptation, that he cannot withstand, springing from his own thwarted needs. And he, who accepted her confession without a word of denunciation, overwhelmed by the miasma, the melancholy of his race which he cannot escape, in his own agony proposes the test,

[1] Both these traits can be found in Ibsen himself. His disappointment over the Danish War was due to his politics being too heroic for practice : and his impressionable nature was the cause of his exile. See above, ch. I, pp. 8–9.

which is to him but a thing of the mind.   At this stage, the action recalls the test of Hedvig propounded by Gregers in *The Wild Duck*.

Rebekke, however, is of this world, and is ready to translate the test into action.   At this final awful revelation of the gap between his dreamer's mind and things as they are, Rosmer at last summons his power to hold doom-session over himself. He, who had thought of suicide, because he saw that his whole life was void and null, now accepts that Rebekke is so much flesh of his flesh that they cannot be judged apart.   " Where I have sinned ", she says, " it is fit I should expiate."   *Kinsmen* in Norwegian are *skyldfolk*, those who share a common guilt. Rosmer's union with Rebekke is so close that he cannot separate her guilt from himself.   He goes with her as Milton's Adam ate the apple, not to be separated from Eve ; yet the effect is not the same.   They do not go to death, after all, to vindicate Rosmer's belief in her.   They go to vindicate their right to each other, by paying blood for blood : and though they have no choice, yet they freely accept their destiny—it is Nietzsche's distinction between negative and positive freedom of the will.

Rebekke : Dost thou faithfully think—that this way is the best ?

Rosmer : I see that it is the only way.

Rebekke : If thou'rt cheating thyself ?   If 'twere only a shadow ? One of the white horses of Rosmersholm ?

Rosmer : It well may be.   For we 'scape them never, we here, of this house.

Rebekke : So bide, Rosmer !

Rosmer : The man shall go with his wife, as the wife with her husband.

Rebekke : Yet tell me first.   Is it thou follows me ?   Or is it I follow thee ?

Rosmer : There we shall never come to rock-bottom.

Rebekke : Yet, still, I wish I could know.

Rosmer : We follow each other, Rebekke.   I, thee ; and thou, me.

Rebekke : I am nigh to thinking that, too.

Rosmer : For now we two are one.
Rebekke : Yes. Now we are one. Come. So we go
joyously. . . .

There is a sense of an intolerable strain being resolved, as in
the union of Antony and Cleopatra.

> *Husband, I come !*
> *Now to that name my courage prove my title.*

Rebekke, who is too often thought of as a mixture of
George Sand and Marie Bashkirtseff, really had more in her
of royal Egypt. She came from Finmark, land of trolls, and
land of witches. "Whom could you not bewitch if you
tried?" groans that sour Puritan, Rektor Kroll. She be-
witches him, and Beate, as well as Rosmer ; but Rosmer
humanizes her until she sees herself for what she is, a " troll
of the sea " clinging to the keel, a mermaid boding shipwreck.
    Rebekke had selected Rosmer because he was impression-
able, as the man she would use to help her " to be with the
new time as it dawned . . . to share all the new beliefs ". But
as Kroll tells her, the new beliefs have not really entered her
blood. Rebekke had strength of will, power of fascination,
but she had no knowledge of herself. And so, in the half-
unwilling way she described, she lured Beate into the millrace,
driven on not by plans for emancipation but by the " wild
craving desire " that had come upon her, for Rosmer. Quick
and fierce as a tigress she acted. And then, Rosmersholm
conquered her. The childlike quality in Rosmer, which
comes out so masterly in his treatment of Brendal, the quality
which is translated " innocence " and which makes men what
Chaucer called " fre "—that generous unsuspecting frankness
which is in some mysterious way so potent a weapon and so
often enables a saint to dominate a crook—thus subdued
Rebekke. Rosmer recruited her into his order of chivalry—
he ennobled her, put her in a new class. Cleopatra fell in
love with Hamlet. This, rather than the intricate manipula-
tions of retrospection, is the core of the play which is no mere
psychological Dance of the Seven Veils. The dead, who

return as rushing white horses over the rushing foam of the millrace, come from Rosmer's past which can be glimpsed but darkly. Rebekke's past is altogether hidden. Yet she is bound by it; she cannot be his wife because of her past, though only her love for him has revealed the significance of the past to her.

> *Rebekke :* That is the horror, that now, when all life's happiness comes to me with full hands—now only can I see, that my own past bars me out.

Rebekke's devotion is absolute. Rosmer dies in the name of justice but Rebekke accepts his verdict for both; she was ready to die for love. He for God only, she for God in him. But it is because of the ancient tradition of justice, the overwhelming respect for law, for " doom ", that is bred in the Norse, that this death seems so fitting and, in a way, so natural. The inevitable is freely chosen; and in this reconciliation of necessity and freedom, in " joyously " paying the price, Rosmer and Rebekke are freed of their guilt of the past. This is not a modern, not an enlightened, not even a rational point of view; for the English equivalent we must go to the Elizabethans at their most Stoic, as in the great last speech of Clermont d'Ambois, or Siward's valediction to his son : " They say he parted well and paid his score."

The strength of Rebekke's character lies in her honesty. In the past, she had led Beate in indirect crooked ways but now she herself faces unflinchingly all the facts as they emerge. It is her hope to be a clear glass to Rosmer, to give him the security of absolute trust. Rosmer's cruellest blow is to tell her she is lying to him.

> *They have most power to hurt us, whom we love :*
> *We lay our sleeping lives within their arms.*

Rebekke loses the power to act and to dare, but her will to be true, to be " trothfast " is unflawed diamond.

I

4

Hedda Gabler is strong in her intellectual dishonesty. She will not face her life, her limitations or her creditors. Hedda has neither self-awareness nor responsibility. Unlike Rebekke and Rosmer she has in their sense no inner life at all : *love* is a word she does not understand and cannot use. There is neither progression nor conflict in her character. From the beginning she is shown as eaten up by envy and pride, in all the malignancy of impotence.[1]

Hedda loathes life. When she sees the cosy affection of Jørgen and Aunt Julle or the mutual trust of Løvborg and Thea she must strike, like a cobra. Her actions are instinctive : she herself admits to Brack that she does not know why she had to " mistake " Aunt Julle's bonnet for the servant's. So, too, she strikes at Løvborg who has forgotten her, and Thea who has supplanted her. " It's now I am burning thy bairn, Thea. Thou, with the curls ! The bairn that is thine and his ! I'm burning it—I'm burning the bairn now ! "

The impulse to murder, which turns inevitably to self-murder, is in itself an inverted form of the life-craving (*livs-kravet*) which had linked Hedda to Løvborg. It is the most primitive form of self-assertion, and frustrated as she is, Hedda is ruled by her militant blood. The cobra strikes, and misses. For each time, her ignorance miscalculates and her attempts to impose her will on circumstances are deflected by some trivial accident in the external fabric of events.

The only person on whom she does get her revenge is

[1] Compare D. H. Lawrence's outburst upon Galsworthy's Irene. " They are parasites upon the thought, the feelings, the whole body of life of really living individuals who have gone before them and who exist alongside them. All they can do . . . is to feed upon the life that has been given by living men to mankind. . . . To keep up a convention needs only the monotonous persistency of the parasite, the endless endurance of the craven, those who fear life because they are not alive. . . . Sneaking and mean Irene prevented June from getting her lover. Sneaking and mean she prevents Fleur. She is the bitch in the manger." *Scrutinies*, ed. Edgell Rickword (Wishart and Co., 1928), pp. 60, 71.

Judge Brack. And perhaps on the unborn child, whose life too is ended by the final pistol shot.

Never is Hedda shown as suffering. She is hardly self-conscious enough to suffer. Although she is once or twice seen alone, there is nothing in the play that could be called a soliloquy from her : she is shown entirely in action. It is a superb acting part : the greatest acting part that Ibsen created because the interpretation is left entirely to the actress, although material is generously provided. The action gives great opportunity and the maximum freedom, since the actress does not have to put across lines of self-analysis or explanation. All that is left to be conveyed in presentation. There is no frame, no comment. No judgment is passed upon Hedda, or even invited. The audience is not asked to respond with a verdict, and this objectivity of presentation, this neutral response is the most discomfiting thing about the play. It was not at all characteristic of the age. Zola or Brieux painted life black enough, but, like the early Ibsen, they invited a judgment : they called aloud for horror or disgust or clinical excitement : they implied a scientific explanation and therefore a potential scientific remedy. Even the least doctrinaire of playwrights will allow moral comment within the frame of the characters. When he drew Iago, Shakespeare allowed the plain man's feeling an outlet in the last outburst of Emilia, and although Iago is a " hollow " character and Emilia is not speaking with any understanding, although the comment may not be taken as the play's full verdict, the balance and rhythm of the whole is built on a consort of such judgments. The counterpoise is even clearer in *Antony and Cleopatra*, in the comments on Cleopatra by Enobarbus and her own attendants.

In *Hedda Gabler* there is no such counterpoise. Jørgen the painful pedant, Løvborg, the debased Dionysius, and Brack, the suave bureaucrat, are equally unpleasant and unimportant, and the two minor women's parts are only " feeds ". If Jørgen showed even that amount of independence which Albany shows in *King Lear*, a scale of reference would be established ; but Hedda more truly than Goneril might say : " My fool usurps my bed." The whole play pivots upon

Hedda but she herself is neither "placed" nor judged. She is a study in a vacuum. Every speech in the play is directed towards the main purpose, the revelation of Hedda's character, although there is no longer the rigid interlocking through implication of speech with speech. As, however, the centre of the play is not a problem but a personality [1] there is less emphasis on the story—on the links of cause and effect. The play proceeds rather by episodic development. Act I gives a full picture of the Tesman ménage and sets out all the main problems. Act II introduces the rivals, Løvborg and Brack, and Hedda's first attempt to play with destiny and to thwart Thea. Act III is given up to the story of the manuscript and ends with Hedda's triumph. Act IV springs the trap, undoes the triumph, and forces Hedda to accept her own counsel and use the second pistol.

Archer noted long ago that the play "raised no special problems", but the fact that it also evokes no emotions, no judgment from the spectators means that there is no longer a tragic catharsis. Rather the attitude is akin to that of *Troilus and Cressida*, a sardonic depth of scepticism where the only satisfaction is to see the biter bit, and the engineer hoist with his own petard. We do not feel, with the final pistol shot, that Hedda has her deserts, nor yet that like Osvald, she is necessity's victim. Whilst unsurpassed technical resources have been brought to bear, there is a kind of arrest or barrier upon the comment, the connexions, the threads which should reach out to ordinary life, its complexities and judgments. For the play is highly selective. Any strong character set up against Hedda would disrupt it : if Eilert Løvborg had been allowed to develop, he might have become positive enough to throw the play out of focus, and so he is used very sparingly and given two hysterical scenes to minimize his force as a character, and prevent any strong feeling for him which would endanger the neutrality of response. He becomes instead a recognizable type, a character eminently to be "used" and not displayed. Aunt Julle, who is worthy yet invites the stinging repartee, rather in the manner of Miss Bates, is also

---

[1] Ibsen himself stressed this point.

eminently to be used. Her character is sufficiently like
Jørgen's to make his constant invoking of her really infuriating
to Hedda. Her simple grief for her sister at the opening of
Act IV, when Hedda has just given the pistol to Løvborg,
and is waiting for the result, is used subtly as perspective to
reveal Hedda's sterility of feeling. Hedda herself is always
being displayed through the other characters and even through
minor passages of interchange and "bridges" between one
scene and another. For example the brilliance and wit of
Hedda's exchange with Brack in Act II, where she fences
with all the zest with which she ever listened to Løvborg's
revelations, come in a transitional scene which could perhaps
be misinterpreted if it were not preceded and coloured by the
opening, in which Hedda cocks her pistol at Judge Brack as
he comes up the garden. Such initial pleasantry corrects any
impression that this is merely a normal flirtation, and colours
all that follows with a sinister light.

We neither dislike nor fear Hedda. We merely assent.
Yes, the traits are recognizable. This feeling of *recognition of
the species* belongs to comedy rather than to tragedy, and
Hedda Gabler has a strong taste of that bitter comedy, the
comedy of *Tartufe* and *Volpone*, which is more purely pessi-
mistic than tragedy.[1] The basis of sardonic comedy is the
theme of the biter bit. Fate is cleverer than Hedda at playing
tricks, and she herself is outplayed at her own game. The
story of her pretended enthusiasm for the Minister's villa is
the first example of it. From sheer boredom and to find a
subject for conversation, she feigned admiration for the house,
as a result of which she finds herself living in it. The final
example is the absurd promptitude with which Thea produces
the rough notes of Løvborg's book, and sets to work on
reconstruction. Archer felt this incident to be shockingly
improbable and so it is. But Thea breathing fervent prayers
that she may inspire Tesman and Tesman hopefully declaring :
" Yes, Hedda, believe it or not—I really think I'm beginning

---

[1] The Works of Marlowe and Jonson are examples of this comedy in
English : there is something of the same tradition, diluted, in *The Beggar's
Opera*.

to feel something like it, now. . . ." are not meant to be
probable. They are acidly comic. Even Hedda's last act,
when she finds the courage she has always lacked and shoots
herself "beautifully" is completely wasted, for no one grasps
its significance.

> *Tesman :* Shot herself ! Shot herself in the head ! Think of
> that !
> *Brack :* But, God bless my soul ! people don't *do* such things !

Hedda Gabler is such very strong meat that, in an age when
the tragic had to be the solemn, its savage comedy was not
appreciated. In his last play Ibsen described how the artist's
portraits really contained hidden portraits of the animal in
man, which no one but he could recognize ; and he adds that
this secret was extraordinarily amusing.[1] *Hedda Gabler* is
the only play of Ibsen to which this description could apply,
and although sardonic comedy is not the only element in the
play—although it is neutralized by excitement and subdued
by realism—it still flavours the play potently. Jørgen, Aunt
Julle and Thea must be allowed to be ridiculous, especially
Thea, who is described unkindly by her creator as being
"pop-eyed". The sharp and merciless comedy should be
more readily perceptible to Ibsen's countrymen ; for there is
in their literature a streak of hardness which finds humour
in situations that are far from pleasant and which turns the
edge of calamity aside by a hardbitten jest.[2] Such asperity
or acerbity of wit, which distinguishes Ibsen even among his
countrymen, was nevertheless also a national inheritance, and
to miss it in *Hedda Gabler* is to blunt the fine edge of the style.
Normally, of course, this attitude goes with a heroic vitality ;
the peculiar and appalling effect in *Hedda Gabler* is that it
accompanies a negative attitude. Nowhere is there the relief
or the recoil which Nietzsche described in *The Genealogy of
Morals*, in which the heroic nature asserts itself against hostility,
instead of attacking directly.

[1] See below, ch. 5, pp. 143-4.
[2] This trait enabled the Norwegians to withstand the German occupation
in such good heart.

We, the happy, we the good, we the fair. . . .[1]

With *Hedda Gabler* Ibsen reached the end of the tether. It is the last of the series that began with *A Doll's House*. The distance between is a measure of what he had achieved. It is on the half-dozen plays of this period that his European fame principally rests, partly because they have the qualities that best survive translation. But his technique was in danger of swamping him. He might easily have collapsed into an imitator of his own past greatness ; he was, after all, sixty-three years of age. He might have followed other men : in *Hedda Gabler* itself there is more than a suggestion of Strindberg, the dramatist whom Ibsen admired most of all among his contemporaries. The savage predatory heroine was Strindberg's invention, and such an incident as the burning of the manuscript is the kind of incident he might have used.

But at this point the work underwent a complete transformation. Ibsen dropped all his " craft so long to lerne ". Although his last plays are written in prose, they are the work of a poet.

This break could only have been the result, perhaps a delayed result, of great inner conflict and tension. The tone of *Hedda Gabler*, at once savage and negative, is near to the border of madness. Hedda herself, as a character, is on the border of madness ; it will depend on the actress whether, at the end of Act III, the border is shown as being crossed. In the last plays it would be irrelevant to think of the characters in such terms. To the rationalist no doubt all the characters in *Bygmester Solness* would be abnormal.

Whatever the inner strain and conflict, we know little about it.[2] Ibsen did not break down. He went back to Norway and exposed himself to his old contacts. That

[1] F. Nietzsche, *The Genealogy of Morals*, First Essay, " The Evil and the Good ", x.

[2] Halvdan Koht is inclined to think that Hedda's denial of life and her bitterness at her own cowardice is not unconnected with Ibsen's love affair with Fraulein Bardach, and when out of discretion he severed the friendship he did feel it as a denial of Dionysus (op. cit., II, p. 257) which is here indirectly reflected. The mood of the play—weariness, barrenness, *tedium vitæ*—probably reflects Ibsen's own, which may have had a variety of causes.

wincing nerve he deliberately bared. Old, famous beyond his contemporaries, honoured by all Europe, he returned after twenty-seven years to Oslo. Every day, carefully dressed in the frock coat and silk hat of respectability, he walked down the Karl Johannes Gate to his café. His clock-work habits, his invincible taciturnity, his intense irritability were confirmed by age and fame. When asked to speak in public he made dry, impersonal speeches ; and at his regular two-yearly intervals he punctually brought out another play. His contemporaries were puzzled by these plays but received them respectfully. Perhaps it was only because he was sardonically aware of how the work would be misunderstood that Ibsen could give to the world these terrible but unfaltering dissections of himself, which make up the last plays.

Not only in a literal sense did Ibsen follow Peer Gynt and obey the voice that cried : " Go back—go back to your home." He went back to the world that Peer went back to, the world of trolls and accusing ghosts. The later plays hark back to the early work, and the early work reflects in an uncanny fashion the history of Ibsen's later days. His work, and his life, are seen at the end to be an indivisible whole.

Chapter Five

THE VISIONARY

" Bygmester Solness " — " Little Eyolf " — " John Gabriel Borkman "—" When we Dead Wake "

AFTER he had finished *Hedda Gabler* Ibsen returned to Norway and for the rest of his life he lived in Oslo. A new and deep change came over his work. The Ibsenites both at home and abroad were puzzled by his last plays ; *Rosmersholm* and *Hedda Gabler* could, with sufficient determination, be interpreted to fit in with preconceived notions of what a play by the author of *A Doll's House* should be like. Extraordinary attempts were made to cope with *Bygmester Solness,*[1] but the later plays were utterly intractable. They were known, however, to be " symbolic " ; but the function of a symbol was by no means clear to the Ibsenites. Respectful and somewhat regretful acceptance of the master's dicta was all that was possible.

When Ibsen returned to Norway he took up the themes that he had dropped at the beginning of his exile—the themes of Hjordis and Skule, of *Love's Comedy* and *On the Vidda,* and his other poems. His analytic, fiercely independent, hard-thinking intellect, his combative and contra-suggestible temper, drew their strength and power from the fixed and tenacious character of his instinctive affections and needs, as mountains are thrown up in an anticline by the opposing thrust of deep-buried strata. Intellectually he was mobile and adaptable, but he was intensely conservative in feeling : a few deep and single experiences shaped him and fixed him. Pedantically exact in habits, with a long memory for injuries and benefits, he maintained an impenetrable reserve towards even his nearest friends. *The lonely one* had been his title from his youth. We know virtually nothing of his own

[1] See below, p. 132.

inner life, except what is told us in his plays. His letters are casual documents, his biographers can throw little light from recollections of relatives or friends.

In Ibsen's later plays the drama springs most directly from his own inner problems and needs. The plays no longer have a plot, they have not, in the old sense, any action at all. There is no clear-cut event where the finality of the physical world intrudes, as when Hedda burns the manuscript, or hands over the pistol. Even death has not the sharp catastrophic force that it had in *Rosmersholm*, but is an inevitable, almost incidental consequence of the state of Life-in-Death which preceded. The background is no longer Norway: it is Eternity. Drama has shifted from Middle Earth to the region of heaven and hell. This brooding introspective writing is the dramatic equivalent of the self-analysis of Kierkegaard; and as he used pseudonyms and parables to enable himself to handle his own feelings and thoughts more delicately and precisely—as a surgeon will use sterilized forceps to pick up a dressing—so Ibsen used his symbols, not to conceal the problem, to wrap it up and make it poetic, as his contemporaries believed; but to isolate and define it. It was but a return to the technique of his early lyrics—*The Miner, The Eider-Duck, Fear of the Light*. A figure like the Rat Wife has more in common with the Button Moulder of *Peer Gynt* than with the characters of the intervening plays; and like the Button Moulder, she is based on a memory of childhood, which for Ibsen, as for Wordsworth, seems largely to have determined the shape of his future experiences.

Ibsen's method, however, went against the main current of the time, as exhibited in the work of his own disciples Brieux and Hauptmann. His symbols of the builder, the miner's son, the sculptor suggest how conscious he was of working in a hard resistant medium: and some words of Rubek may be applied to himself: "Yes, is not life in sunshine and in beauty a hundred times better worth while than to hang about to the end of your days in a raw damp hole, and struggle with lumps of clay and blocks of stone?"

The medium was resistant because the substance of what

Ibsen had to say was so remote and intangible ; there were no ready-made concepts for what he wished to speak of, either in his own work or elsewhere. He had to make a completely new start.

The four last plays of Ibsen are as sharply divided from his earlier work as the four last plays of Shakespeare. And, like Shakespeare, Ibsen seems in these plays to present not a conflict but a vision of good and evil. He uses the dramatic form because it was second nature to him ; but the craftsmanship that was bred into his bone is seen only in the minor aspects of the plays—they are no longer perfectly tempered. They are the vehicle for the artist's vision of " the small circle of pain within the skull ". The inward vision becomes sharper each time, but the power of the dramatic artist declines. The plays are written in descending order of dramatic greatness. In the last work—which is not a play in the ordinary sense at all—Ibsen holds his final doom-session over himself, and ends with a personal testament, so bitter a repudiation and palinode of all he had done that, having produced it, he was stricken helpless and silent.[1] Nevertheless *When we Dead Wake* is terrible and pitiful only as Ibsen's last testament : it requires to be read as spiritual auto-biography, whereas *Bygmester Solness* stands by itself as a great work though it gains immensely when placed in relation to the rest of Ibsen's writing.

In all four plays the theme is remorse of conscience. The choice that was made in *Love's Comedy*, *On the Vidda*, and *Brand*, is seen, across the interval of thirty years, to have been the wrong choice. That impulse to sacrifice, which had seemed so noble, is given its real name—murder. The

[1] Archer held that the play is symptomatic of the coming break-down, but it seems far more likely that the breakdown was a consequence of the strain of writing the play. Halvdan Koht says " Ibsen held his final reckoning with himself in the play which he made the Epilogue to his life work. . . . Its inner relation with all the last dramas is clear enough : the same funda-mental question fills them all. But *When we Dead Wake* has much more strongly than the others received the stamp of an account with himself. . . . Only in *Love's Comedy* can we find anything of the same kind. Nor had he written anything so personal since *Love's Comedy* " (II, pp. 321-2).

murder of love, and its fruit, the child—of Solness's children, of his wife's living happiness, of Eyolf, of Ella's power to love, of Irene's power to love, of Rubek's power to create and of their child, his vision—these are the doom that follows when, in however great a cause, the kindly virtues of mutual love are rejected. Nor is restitution possible. Recognition of the wrong choice kills. Solness perishes in the moment when he plants the garland, Borkman is slain by the icy air of the heights, Rubek and Irene are overwhelmed in an avalanche, as Brand was overwhelmed. But death on the heights is preferable to life-in-death down below; and the more heroic virtue is to turn and face the consequences of the wrong choice, to go back to the heights at any cost, and to die facing in the right direction.

Bygmester Solness is " a cloud-castle with a good groundwork down below ". The characters have a new kind of strength and life, because Ibsen found a new way to make them speak. The new development is first and foremost a literary development.

In this play Ibsen succeeds in doing what few dramatists except Shakespeare can do; each character has his own idiom, his own particular accent, so that the whole dialogue is impregnated with direct dramatic significance. It is common enough to produce characters who have some individuality of speech, especially in comedy. Stensgård, Engstrand and Stockmann are early examples in Ibsen's work. But Shakespeare and Ibsen can make the lightest word so inevitably in character that without need for the conscious implication of *A Doll's House* or the retrospective complexities of *Rosmersholm* every word can bear directly on the revelation of what the play is *about*, every word can have structural as well as local force.

Bygmester Solness has this fecundity and colour of idiom in pre-eminence. Solness's character is given in his speech, in his growls and hasty oaths, his vehement outbursts, his pounces of irascibility, which render directly his passionate struggle for life against the creeping paralysis of fear and remorse that is seizing him. Hilde's usual speech is an excited

and slangy gallop : her characteristic cry is " Straks ! "—
" Now this minute ! " but her vivid changes of mood are
reflected in sudden metaphors—" our cloud-castle . . ." " I
have come out of a grave. . . ." Aline's pitiful clipped
brevities, her parrot-like repetition of " It is my duty ",
would become monotonous if her part were longer. The
difference in achievement between a distinct idiom like
Solness's and that of, say, Hjalmer Ekdal, is that Solness has
heights and depths to range and that, throughout, his tone
and accent remains recognizably the same, whether he is
bullying the Broviks or confessing the torture of watching
others flayed alive to feed his ambition. His speech can rise
till, like that of the great Elizabethan characters, it becomes
the full voice, the total exposition of the play : yet it does
not cease to be Solness who speaks. The earlier characters
are much simpler, much less faceted than he is.

The play is a triptych—two minor active passages, Acts I
and III, being set each side of the great lyric centrepiece,
which is virtually a duet between Solness and Hilde. The
first act itself has three divisions : Solness and the Broviks,
Solness and the Doctor, and Solness and Hilde. As usual,
Ibsen began his construction very carefully, but when he got
into his stride, his planning was no longer so obvious.

In the first act, we see Solness as the successful, tempera-
mental artist. He changes his mind unfairly; he domineers and
exploits ; but his energy makes it inevitable that he should.
Beside him, the Broviks have no chance. With the doctor,
however, he is uneasy. He betrays his fear of retribution—

Solness : Early or late, it makes me afraid—desperately afraid.
    For the luck will turn, you know——

his fear of youth, his fear of his own madness.

With Hilde, youth comes into the play, gay, careless and
confident. Her confidence braces Solness, her insouciance
amuses him. But then, as the dialogue between them runs
deeper, an enchantment comes over the speech. Their words
are but common words, and yet the two are being swept
along—and their clutching at trivialities betrays that they
know it—by an undertow that they cannot resist.

Solness: Yes . . . today is the nineteenth of September too.

Hilde: Yes, it is. . . . And the ten years are up. And you did not come—as you promised.

Solness: It is a wonderful thing. Yet the more I think of it all, the more it comes to me, that in all these long years I have gone about in torment trying to . . . to . . .

Hilde: What?

Solness: To find something—some kind of great moment that I felt I had had, and lost. But never could I find the clue to what it could have been.

Hilde: You should have put a knot in your handkerchief, Bygmester.[1]

Solness: Then I should only have had to go about pondering, what the knot could mean.

Hilde: Ah yes . . . there are trolls in the world, to be sure.

Solness: It is wonderfully good that you came to me.

Hilde: Is it good, do you think?

and to Hilde's twice repeated cry: " Can't you make use of me, Bygmester?" he says: " You are that, of which I have sorest need."

Never, it should be noted, do these two use the intimate *Du* to each other. It is *De* throughout and to the end. Never does a word of endearment pass. In the second act, a sustained love duet in the manner of *Tristan*, Solness may use the similes of a lover, but he does not use his tone.

Solness: You are like the dawn of the day. When I look at you, I seem to look towards the sunrise.

Hilde: Tell me, Bygmester, don't you think you must have called me to you? Called me secretly?

Solness: I almost think I must have done.

Hilde: What do you want of me?

Solness: You are Youth, Hilde. Youth itself.

[1] Hilde's mode of address is usually translated *Mr. Solness*. This is too stiff. She says *Bygmester* as we should say *Doctor*. It suits her relation to him exactly. Norwegian has much greater precision of designation, e.g. Engineer Borgheim, Student Erhart Borkman, Squire (Landowner) Ulfheim, etc. Not Mr. Borgheim, Mr. Borkman.

Hilde : Youth, that you are so afraid of ?
Solness : And that draws me so powerfully and deeply.

She is in love with greatness, as he is in love with youth :
like Falk and Svanhild, they are not in love with each other.
It is the vision of Solness on top of the tower that she sees,
not the sick and ageing builder : the fact of his cruelty to
Ragnar distresses her less than the motive for it.

Solness : Hopeless, Hilde. The luck will turn against me some
   day. Sooner or later. Justice can't be turned from its course.
Hilde : Don't talk like that ! Do you want to take my life ?
   To take what is *more* than my life ?
Solness : What is more than your life ?
Hilde : To see you great. To see you with a garland in your
   hand. High, high up on a church spire.

The remorse of Solness is incomprehensible to Hilde, a
morbidity of conscience ; but she herself has an instinctive
sympathy with everyone she meets. She says exactly what
she thinks, and acts instantly on her impulses, whether or not
they happen to be contradictory. She does not understand
Solness's feeling that he has built his success at the price of
murder, yet she herself is ready to leave after her talk with
Aline, she pities the Broviks, and might even pity Solness,
could she see him detached from her vision. In the last act
Hilde flashes from mood to mood—sympathy, jealousy, the
fierceness of the " bird of prey " when her troll is in possession.
Solness's anguish of confession is partly lost on her, and he
is really not addressing her in person ; he is unburdening
himself.

Solness : I can tell you what it feels like to have the luck on your
   side ! It feels like a great open wound on my breast ! And
   the allies and servants are for ever flaying pieces of skin off
   others, to close my wound ! But still the wound is not
   healed ! Never ! Never !

She may seem to pity and understand, because she, like he,
has a troll in her and understands the state of being possessed.
But she cannot enter into his fear of youth and of retribution,

because she is "the dawning of the day". She supports him, by refusing to recognize his fears, and by temporarily exorcizing them.

The revelation of Solness in Act II and III is made only through Hilde and not to her : he uses her as a confessional. The story of the fire which ruined his life and made him the sort of artist he is is told simply : [1] but the second confession about the " allies and servants "—that he *willed* to start the fire—is an appeal to the troll in her.   Then there are interludes of exquisite crossplay between the two, culminating in her indirect confession of her love.   Again, Solness drops into character, and becomes the grumbling elderly artist and Hilde deftly coaxes him into signing the " damned drawings " of Brovik.   He blazes up at the end in a measured affirmation of renewed strength : " Tomorrow then we will plant the garland . . . Princess Hilde "[2]—only to sink in ominous diminuendo :

Hilde : Over your new home, yes.
Solness : Over the new house.   It will never be home to me.

He cannot forget the price of being the master builder.

It is not till the last act that Solness finally confesses his challenge to God on the tower, and how he had refused to be the kind of artist he might have been—and become a lesser kind of artist.   This is why he fears the heights and fears retribution.   He has hid that one talent which is death to hide.   He finds too that his art is worthless after all—and the happiness he had sacrificed for it equally worthless.   This is the nadir of the play.

Solness : That—to build homes for human beings—is not worth a brass farthing, Hilde.
Hilde : Do you think so, now ?
Solness : Yes.   For now I see it is true.   Humanity has no use

[1] The fire that burnt down the old house, it will be remembered, is the first test of the artist in *On the Vidda.*

[2] " Ikvaeld hejser vi altså kransen—prinsesse Hilde."   The verb (usually translated *hang*) means *hoist* and is used e.g. of running up a flag.   Solness is preparing to nail his colours.

for this kind of home. Nor any use for happiness, none at all. And I should have had no use for such a home. Even if I could have had one. So that's the upshot of it all, as far back as I can get. Nothing built—basically, nothing. And nothing sacrificed for the building either. Nothing, nothing —anywhere.

It is the cry of Borkman and of Rubek—" We see that we have never really lived." Both as artists, and as men, they fail. Yet, after all this, Solness dies triumphantly; he " achieves the impossible " and faces again his fearful Jahweh, not as artist, but as a man.

> *Solness :* I will say, Hear me, thou Almighty Lord : and judge me according to Thy decrees. But hereafter I will build only the most enchanting and lovely thing of all. . . .

It is this which Hilde hears as " harps in the air " sounding [1] and cries

> *Hilde :* There is One with him, that he disputes with. . . . I hear a song. A mighty song. . . . Ah, wave up to him ! For now, now the building is done !

Then he falls. He had climbed, intoxicated by Hilde's ardour, as she, intoxicated by the fulfilment of her vision, waves and cries and finally brings him down. Whenever they are together, she can fire him by a word, a challenge and, like the bird of prey, she is reckless of what happens then to him. This is the only kind of union they can achieve : he is age and she is youth, but when " the impossible lures and beckons " they both see, momentarily, the same vision. It is a castle in the air ; a mirage, with no foothold for the master builder ; but to have seen the castle is worth the price of the fall.

Solness must not be equated with Ibsen. " He is a man who is somewhat akin to me," Ibsen admitted cautiously.[2] Ibsen had often called himself a builder, and long ago in his

---

[1] Is there an echo of this in the famous last line of *The Cherry Orchard* ?
[2] Koht, II, p. 301.

K

youth he had written the poem *Building Plans* which seems like a first glimpse of this play. Ibsen himself, too, suffered from the physical fear of heights which he gave to the master builder: he dared not look downwards into chasms. As for the fear of the younger generation, he had heard himself openly attacked by the young rising novelist, Knut Hamsun, and world-famous as he was, his sensitive vanity must have been wounded very near the quick.[1] But the attempt to turn this visionary play into a *roman à clef* is as crass as the attempt of the unlucky Fräulein Barduch to appropriate to herself the title Princess of Orangia. Ibsen, not very politely, contradicted her. His contemporaries, of course, produced the most amazing explanations. "Solness was taken for a picture of Bjørnson, of Bismarck, or of Gladstone ; and Hilde was interpreted as the morality of the future given flesh and blood."[2] Archer enquires earnestly whether Solness were a hypnotist or not, and ponders precisely at what point in Ibsen's published work he ceased to build churches with high towers and started to build homes for humanity. Such literalism must have been infuriating to Ibsen, and in his last play he allows himself a cutting reference.[3] The Ibsenites were still thinking in terms of *A Doll's House* and *Ghosts*.

On one or two occasions, the writing seems to falter. In the last act there is too much carpentry, too much of Brovik, and the Doctor, Aline's duty, and Hilde's jealousy. The physical side of the accident is as irrelevant as the end of *Cymbeline*, but with a sufficiently dominant Hilde, the cries and swoons and everyday details can be reduced to a background. Partly, of course, the difficulty lay in the representational stage of the day, which did not allow Ibsen to use a convention here.

Detail of everyday life, however, is of small account in *Bygmester Solness*. "The power and the glory", as Ibsen would have said, lay elsewhere, in Solness's and Hilde's great speeches, in the remorse of the artist who realizes not only that he has destroyed himself and others for his art, but has misused that art itself; and then, when it is too late, is over-

[1] Koht, II, pp. 288–9.   [2] ibid., II, p. 310.   [3] See below, p. 143.

taken by the instinct for life—" the lovely earth-life " as
Irene calls it. Solness's energy and desperate need blaze up
like a vast conflagration. Yet Ibsen ran his own molten
experience into a mould, made a play out of it ; this implies
a discipline which means that he was not merely a Solness.
He remained a builder. This part of the experience is necessarily left out of the play, because it was what called the play
into being.

2

Little Eyolf, the next play, is written in a style which is
completely the antithesis of *Bygmester Solness*. The characters
of *Bygmester Solness* are strong, violent, vivid, because their
idiom makes them so. *Little Eyolf* is mostly written in a
monotone which invests all the characters with a grey and
chilly remoteness. The sentences are all short, so short that
there is a feeling of disjointed ejaculation about everything
that is said. Ibsen never used the negative qualities of style
with such consistency before. This flatness and absence of
emotion, however, isolates more sharply the nature of the
new experience. It is one which perhaps was rare among the
Ibsenites, but is not generally unfamiliar—conversion. A long
period of frustration, seeking, emotional sterility suddenly ends
in security, health, emotional release. Such experiences are
not inevitably religious.[1] But they come only to reflective
men :

> *Those to whom the miseries of the world*
> *Are misery, and will not let them rest,*

as Keats described them in the prelude to his own Vision.
    In setting and background, the play has much in common
with *The Sea Woman*. The calm empty places in the moun-

---

[1] It was not so, e.g., in the case of John Stuart Mill. The classical account
of conversion is still William James's *Varieties of Religious Experience*. Since
this paragraph was written, Miss Una Ellis Fermor in *The Frontiers of Drama*
(Methuen, 1945), p. 21, has observed, " Ibsen's *Master Builder*, *Rosmersholm*
and other of his latest plays are all plays of conversion."

tains, the calm long windings of the fjord, so powerful and so deadly, throw up the tiny human figures against their grand monotony. The Rat Wife, a memory from Ibsen's childhood, blends into the countryside a supernatural lure and call, like that of Ellida's sailor, the warlock from Finmark. Like Ellida, Allmers can see the steamer sailing away down the fjord and so out into the world, while he sits alone, and tries to invent duties for himself.

Because of the stylized speech and the rich local values of the setting, in Norway *Little Eyolf* is probably actable, as some of the embroidered legendary plays of Yeats or Synge are here. It would be slow and loaded, but it could be put across. *Little Eyolf*—at least in the existing translations—is not an actable play in English. The characters have not the vigour which makes *Bygmester Solness* such a great and dangerous opportunity for the actor. The whole mood of the play belongs to the Norwegian background. The sense of brooding melancholy, the feeling of physical and spiritual isolation can be met again and again in the literature of the country. The mood is bred of the living. Even Borgheim, the exception to this, is significant by reason of his profession —he is a road-builder " What a joy to be a road-builder ! " he cries at one point. Roadmaking is not a particularly significant occupation in England. But in Norway, where the new roads of the nineteenth century transformed the countryside, linking together by a few hours' travel, places that had been a day's sea journey apart, where nearly every road was an engineering feat of tunnelling, bridging, banking —the roadmaker was a symbol of progress in a very precise sense. His was a social service of such obvious value that he might become a storm-centre of local politics. Even today, the prospect of a new road or railway in the remoter parts of Norway will stir up local feuds and parties to something almost approaching their ancient strength. In giving Borgheim this occupation, therefore, Ibsen has endowed him with the kind of qualities that in our literature are associated with the Empire Builders of Kipling, and contrasted him in the strongest possible manner with Allmers, the student of philosophy with his unwritten book on Human Responsibility.[1]

The first act of *Little Eyolf* is the most dramatic, with the caressing and slimy wheedling of the Rat Wife, her boasted power of luring her lovers to death and her sinister familiar, the little black dog. Allmers says, when she has gone, " I can well understand the resistless, luring power she talked of. The loneliness up among the peaks and on the great *vidda* has something of that," linking her with his own strange experience among the mountains. In the second part of Act I, the passionate scene between Rita and Allmers is more in the style of *Hedda Gabler*, a savage analysis of a predatory woman, as terrifying in her craving for love as Hedda in her craving for life. But Rita has lost the power to lure, and even though Allmers does not yet openly invoke " the law of change ", it is seen in its effects.

Act II is in effect a threnody, and like the central act of *Bygmester Solness*, it carries the main weight of the play. Remorse and retribution are its theme—*gengaeldelse*—the old dread of Solness, of Rebekke, of Mrs. Alving, the rule of the ghosts. " There was retribution in little Eyolf's death. Doom over thee and me," says Allmers. Rita and Allmers shrank from Eyolf because they felt guilty of his lameness. Their sorrow for him was not pure grief but only remorse. When Allmers dreamt that Little Eyolf was alive and no longer lame, he praised God. But in his waking hours he does not believe in God. Hence he cannot ask forgiveness, and he dares not forgive himself.

The story of Asta is not irrelevant, but it seems at times to be part of the carpentry, and to be given too much prominence. In his sister Allmers found all the support his wife and child could not give him, in a calmer, more limpid affection ; Asta gives Allmers what Hedvig gave Hjalmer.[2] Eyolf and Asta have also a mysterious affinity and affection

---

[1] Solness too belonged to a class which transformed Norway. The replacing of the old wooden houses, which still give such charm to the quays, by modern buildings, effected a domestic revolution in Norway.

[2] Is it a coincidence that they both, possibly, are illegitimate ?

for each other, as well as the secret fact of their name in common : but even as Eyolf turns out to have been "a little stranger boy", so Asta turns out not to be of Allmer's blood [1] and both are lost to him.

The last act, which solves all the problems, is probably the least successful. Allmer's dream, which might serve as an illustration for a description of "rebirth" in a psychological textbook, the hoisting of the flag, the final exhortation to "look towards the mountain peaks and the great silence" are not organically related to what went before. Both Rita and Allmers have confessed that they belong to "the life of earth", that they cannot find consolation in exaltation. Allmers feels it his duty to grieve continually for Little Eyolf, but catches himself wondering what there will be for lunch. Yet in the last act, this irony, which turns even their deepest feelings to something ludicrous and mean, which flavours their remorse with petty distaste, is all dissolved away. The fear that bereavement was making them not nobler but "more evil and distorted" has lapsed, and there is almost a pious suggestion that Little Eyolf did not die in vain. The solution is quite effective, it is probably, like that of *The Sea Woman*, psychologically accurate, but it is not dramatically convincing. The power of the play lies in the dramatic episodes of Act I and the "visionary dreariness" of Act II.

Ibsen made several slighting references to Allmers in his letters—"this feeble, infatuated person". Allmers does not see his own motives clearly : he has lived on theories and good intentions. In fact he has more than an unwritten book and dependence on his womenfolk in common with Hjalmer : yet his grief is taken seriously. But the attitude towards him remains rather dubious, and as he is the central figure this leaves the whole intention blurred. Rita, a simpler and more violent character, is entirely shattered by the catastrophe. She can no longer fight to keep Allmers ; but it is she who first reaches the solution. She must put something

---

[1] Rita is jealous of Asta's power over Eyolf, as Gunhild Borkman of her sister's power over Erhard. In his later plays Ibsen seems especially interested in what might be called oblique relationships.

in Eyolf's place. First it is to be Asta—then the village children. Her motives are humble. She will look after them, not because she is convicted of sin, but because she has nothing else to do. It is she, and not Allmers, who is really haunted by the child's memory. No thoughts of lunch obliterate for her the cry "The crutch is floating!" (*Krykken flyder!*). This picture is quite consistent, but again it is not really related to the insatiate harpy of Act I, who is a link between Hedda Gabler and Gunhild Borkman. It seems that the dominant note of Act II, the feeling of remorse and vacancy, which is conveyed so marvellously by the toneless, halting rhythm, has dominated the character. The play is indeed one in which examination of detail profits little. The broad sweeping effects obliterate local distinction and it has less plot, in both the important and the unimportant senses, than any of Ibsen's plays except the last.

3

John Gabriel Borkman and *When we Dead Wake* are so closely linked that they may almost be called alternative statements of a single theme. But whereas the writing of *John Gabriel Borkman* is vehement and passionate, *When we Dead Wake* is written in a neutral style. Both plays are devoid of the "uncompromising solid objects" of Ibsen's middle period. All that has fallen away. The characters are no longer seen "in the round", they no longer modify one another or develop. Each stands alone, a centre of dereliction and despair. The unveiling of their past motives or the hidden consequences of their acts does not produce a new situation as it does for Rebekke or even Rita. Remorse, grief, memory that is suffering, and memory that is beyond suffering rule them. To recognize their state of life-in-death is physically mortal ; yet redemption lies only in such recognition.[1] There is no change, no reversal, but only a disavowal which can lead nowhere because it comes too late.

[1] Recognition, *anagnorisis* should rightly be the culmination of the plot. Here, however, it is the whole play.

Borkman and Rubek have been guilty of the same crime, and are accused by Ella and Irene in almost the same words.

Ella : It is thou hast sinned. Thou put to death all the human joy that ever I had. All the woman's joy at least. From that day that thy shape began to dwindle, I've lived my life eclipsed in shadow. During all these years it's grown harder and harder for me—and now it's impossible—to love any thing alive. No man, no beast, no growing plant even . . .

Irene : I went into the darkness when the child stood in the radiance of the light . . . I gave thee my young, living soul. So I stood all empty within . . . soulless. . . . It was that I died of, Arnold. . . . The power of love is dead in me.

Borkman sold his love for " all the hidden, golden spirits " and Rubek his because he was " first and foremost an artist ". " The work of art comes first," retorts Irene, " and flesh and blood next." He does not deny it. By this betrayal, Borkman and Rubek each severed the artery of their own power. Too late, they feel the pangs of living.

Borkman : No, no ! I have been so close to death, so very close. But now I have wakened. I am restored. My life still lies before me . . .

Gunhild : Dream no more of life. Stay quietly, there where thou lies dead.

Irene : Suddenly it came to me with horrible clearness—that thou wert dead long ago.

Rubek : Dead ?

Irene : Dead. Dead, like me. We sat there by the Taunitz Lake, we two clay-cold corpses, and played together. . . . The love that belongs to the life of earth—the lovely, enchanting life of earth—the mysterious life of earth—is dead in us both.

There are innumerable echoes between the two plays. Ella calls herself and Gunhild " two shadows ". Irene says, " I have become my own shadow." Borkman promises Ella " the power and the glory " from the mountain height, as

Rubeck has promised Irene and Maia that they should see
" all the glory of the world ".[1] The final scenes of death
on the heights correspond very closely.

But while the themes are closely related, the treatment is
very different. *John Gabriel Borkman* has a conventional
setting and an exciting story. There is dramatic power in
the fight between the twin sisters in Act I—so quick and
intimate, so hot and close and frank, it recalls the earliest history
plays, the *flyting* of Hjørdis and Gudrun. Ella and Gunhild,
angel and demon, are twins : yet each lives out her tragedy
alone, and though the contest is exciting, it does not lead
anywhere—that is to say there is no real relationship between
the two.

> *Ella :* That is only a thing thou'lt dream of : for had thou not
> that to hold fast to, thou'st be in despair.
>
> *Gunhild :* Yes, then I should despair altogether. And perhaps
> that's what thou wouldst like, Ella.
>
> *Ella :* Yes, I should—better than thou should free thyself by
> trampling on Erhard.
>
> *Gunhild :* Thou'lt thrust thyself between us ! Between mother
> and son ! Thou wilt !
>
> *Ella :* I'll free him from thy power—thy will—thy domination.
>
> *Gunhild :* Thou canst do that no longer. Thou hadst him in
> thy mesh—till he was fifteen. But now I have him again,
> sithee !
>
> *Ella :* Then I will win him back once more. We two, we've
> fought to the death for a man before, Gunhild—we have an'
> all !

Gunhild, more savagely possessive than Rita, more cold
and repellent than Aline, has an icy power as great as that
of the hidden golden spirits that enslave her husband, and
which she uses in the service of her idol Duty. Yet the
suffering she inflicts is less than what she endures. She listens
in silence to the footsteps of the husband, whom she will

---

[1] This phrase occurs as early as *Kingmaking*, where the ghost of Bishop
Nicholas uses it to Skule in Act V. There is little doubt that Ibsen had
the Temptation in mind.

not see—this is one of the great *theatrical* moments of the play, one of the few occasions on which Ibsen really is thinking in terms of the stage.[1]

> *Gunhild :* Time and again it comes over me that I have a sick wolf loping in a cage up there in the long gallery. It lies right overhead. Canst thou only hearken ! Hark ! To and fro . . . to and fro . . . lopes the wolf.

Another such moment is when the sleigh bells are heard bearing Erhard away, and Ella in pity cries to her enemy :

> *Ella :* Gunhild if thou'lt cry out after him, cry now ! Perhaps after all . . . Hurry, Gunhild ! Now they are passing right under us, below.
>
> *Gunhild :* No. I'll not cry out after him. Let Erhard Borkman pass me by. Far, far away, to what he calls life and joy.
>
> *Ella :* Now we hear the bells no longer.
>
> *Gunhild : I thought they sounded like a funeral bell.*

Yet there is also a good deal of carpentry in this play. That indeed is its weakness. The Foldals, left over from an older play, are fitted in with neatness and care but they are unnecessary, like the fussy detail of Erhard and Mrs. Wilton's elopement, the shadowy Heinkels, and the maid. A parlour-maid in the Inferno would be as much in place as this little *stuepige* in the last scene. The cleverly manœuvred exposition, the cunning withholding of John Gabriel himself till Act II, and the melodramatic end to that act are less openly incongruous, but the core of the play is a rough draft of a lyric on the curse of power, the unredeemable past, the hunger pangs of love. Like *The Sea Woman*, this play has a poetic centre which is not related to, and in some sense conflicts with the structural pattern of action and characters. The great speeches of Ella and Borkman in Act II and his hymn to the spirits of the mine in Act IV are high flights which gain little from their context. They are poetry but not drama. John Gabriel's first words are of his cold dark kingdom but they are incongruously addressed to little Freda Foldal.

[1] There is a similar scene in Strindberg's *The Father* (1887).

Borkman : I was a miner's son. And my father took me with him down into the mine. Down there the metal sings. As it is loosed. The hammer blow that loosens it, that is the midnight bell that strikes and sets it free. Therefore it sings . . . in joy . . . after its kind. For it will come up into the light of day and serve men.

The Banker is a miner's son. John Gabriel sees power in concrete terms—almost sensuously. But this power he must have, this kingdom he must win. This is the fatal Fafner's hoard, the troll's treasure for which he sells himself. The enchanting power of the golden spirits is fatal. Yet Borkman is so deeply bound that even at the end he scarcely sees what he has lost.

Borkman : My kingdom. The kingdom I held myself ready to enter—that time I—that time I—died.

Ella : Ah, John ! John !

Borkman : And now it lies fenceless, lordless—open to robbers' conquest and plunder ! Ella ! Dost thou see the mountain chain yonder—far away ? One behind the other. They rise. They tower. That is my deep, boundless, unfathomable kingdom.

Ella : Ah, but the breath from that kingdom is so icy cold, John.

Borkman : That breath is a life-breath to me ! That breath comes to me as a salutation from the obedient subject spirits. I see them, the fast-bound millions. I feel the veins of ore, as they stretch their bending, branching, luring arms out, after me ! I saw them before me, shades that lived and moved, that night when I stood in the bank vaults with the candle in my hand. . . . You longed to be free ! And I tried to free you ! But I had not the power. The treasure hoard sank back into the earth again. . . . But I will whisper to you in the silence of the night. I love you, as you lie, stifled and dead, in the deep and the gloom. I love you, life-craving beings—with all your shining company of power and glory ! I love you, love you, love you !

In this vision of the kingdom and the power and the glory, there is nothing left for the actor or the action ; it sums up the play but it is hardly dependent on the play—certainly not dependent at all on the loves of Erhard, the duel of Ella and Gunhild, or the speech of Ella, which follows, and in turn sums up her story :

> *Ella :* Yes, thy love still stays down there, John. It has always been there. But here up in the day—here was a living warm human heart that beat and throbbed for thee. And that heart thou crushed. Ah, worse than that. Ten times worse. Thou sold it. . . .

There is tremendous force in this play. The main characters are among the most striking Ibsen ever drew, the situations are strong even to melodrama, but the power is not harnessed. Ibsen knew, after this, that what he wanted to write was a poem, or an autobiography. He spoke of both, but the faculty was not in him. He struggled for three years and then produced his last word—not a play, though cast in dramatic form, but rather an apocalyptic *Masque of Life* in which he tried finally and consistently to embody his vision.

4

When we Dead Wake (published November, 1899) was written slowly and painfully, and barely finished when Ibsen collapsed. As Koht said, " It is his own life problem which trembles and vibrates through the play, almost without concealment or change."[1] Rubek the artist is more bitterly condemned than either Solness or Borkman had been. Irene, the " woman risen from the dead ", is an accusing phantom ; Maia and Ulfheim are only lay figures in illustration of his doom.

> *Let me disclose the gifts reserved for age*
> *To set a crown upon your lifetime's effort.*
> *First, the cold friction of expiring sense*
> *Without enchantment, offering no promise*

[1] Koht, II, p. 322.

But bitter tastelessness of shadow fruit
As body and soul begin to fall asunder.
Second, the conscious impotence of rage
At human folly, and the laceration
Of laughter at what ceases to amuse. . . .
And last the rending pain of re-enactment
Of all that you have done, and been : the shame
Of motives late revealed and the awareness
Of things ill done and done to others' harm
Which once you took for exercise of virtue
Then fools' approval stings, and honour stains. . . .[1]

These lines of T. S. Eliot seem completely to sum up the
experience which is presented through the character of Rubek.
The desolate clarity which exposes his loss to him is itself
the power of the artist ; and this is all that his gift is now
good for. For Rubek has lost the key to his art : he has
finally lost the power to create. He despises his own work,
and still more the people who hail it as great.

Rubek : When I had finished this masterpiece of mine :—for
the Resurrection Day is a masterpiece ! Or was at first !
No, it is one still ! A masterpiece it shall and must be ! It
must ! It must !
Maia : Why, the whole world knows that, Rubek.
Rubek : The whole world knows nothing ! Understands
nothing !
Maia : Still, they may guess something.
Rubek : Something of a kind that never was there, yes ! Something that never was in my thoughts ! That they can be ecstatic
about ! (growling). There's no good in going about knocking
oneself up for Tom, Dick and Harry—for the " whole
world ".

Perhaps it was self-protection which led the critics to dismiss
this play as a dotage. Rubek goes on :

Rubek : There is something mysterious—something hidden and
behind all these portraits—something secret that no man can

[1] T. S. Eliot, *Four Quartets*, pp. 39–40.

see. Only I can see it. And it's exceedingly amusing.
Superficially there's the striking likeness that they all stand
and gape at—but deep underneath there are noble honourable
horse-faces, and obstinate donkey-muzzles, and lop-eared,
villainous-low dogs' skulls and greasy hogs' snouts—and the
slack, brutal fronts of the horned herd as well—

Maia : All the dear old farmyard in fact.

Rubek : Just the dear old farmyard, Maia.[1]

At one point Rubek had really given up art in favour of
life. That was why he married Maia, "because all the talk
about the artist's vocation and so on, sounded very empty
and hollow" as he tells her. But it did not succeed, for
Maia cannot share his thoughts, and he finds after all he must
go on working and that he is still inevitably an artist. Then
Irene, the one and only source of his achievement, comes
back to him from "the world beyond the grave", with her
double accusation. He had taken her young life and used it
as raw material for his art ; and then he had thrown her
aside. She loved him : she was made to bear real children,
not merely to be the instrument of his art, even though the
statue was their child, and born of them both.

Rubek : I was an artist, Irene.

Irene : That is it. That is it.

Rubek : First and foremost an artist. . . . The supersti-
tion held me that if I touched thee, if I desired thee sensuously,
my soul would be profaned so that I would be unable to
achieve that which I strove for. And I still think there was
truth in that.

Irene : The work of art comes first : and flesh and blood next.

Rubek : Thou must judge me as thou wilt. But at that time
I was under the power of my work. And it filled me with
glorious joy.

---

[1] It should be remembered that Ibsen was a caricaturist, and that in his
childhood he was caught laughing to himself at the thought of the ugly faces
he *might* have been drawing. He did draw animal caricatures as a journalist
and the *Balloon Letter to a Swedish Lady*, a poem about his visit to Egypt in
1869, described all the envoys under animal figures. Trolls were sometimes
depicted with animals' heads.

So he could drop Irene when the " child " was finished, and
he even forgot her, because he " willed to forget ". But
without Irene he lost the vision, and degraded the statue with
the animals' faces of his farmyard. Irene is ready to kill him
at that word, and crouches behind him with drawn knife.

Irene : There thou pronounced doom over thyself. . . .
Rubek : Doom ?
Irene : My whole soul—thine and mine—we, we and our child
were in that single figure.

This is the second stage of Rubek's enlightenment. And
when he describes how he added his own figure—" I call it
Remorse for a Wasted Life "—she says bitterly :

Irene : Poet ! Thou'rt slack and slothful, and full of forgiveness
of sin for all thy own misdeeds and thoughts. Thou killed
my soul—and thou'lt model thyself in remorse and repentance
and gloom—and then thou thinks thy reckoning is squared.

And while Maia the bird of prey[1] goes off with her bearkiller,
Squire Ulfheim, Rubek suddenly sees that he has rejected
both life and art in casting off Irene when he had " no further
use for her ".

Rubek : A summer night on the *vidda*. With thee ! With
thee ! Ah, Irene, that could have been our life. And that
we have lost—we two.
Irene : We see the irretrievable only when——
Rubek : Yes ?
Irene : When we dead wake.
Rubek : Yes, what do we see then ?
Irene : We see, that we have never lived.

In the last act, on the peaks and in the storm, Maia and
Ulfheim, the rejected ones, " draw their rags together " and
seek safety in the valley, and Irene tells Rubek that it is too
late to live : " the lovely life of earth " is dead in them both.

[1] This phrase suggests, what her general portrayal confirms, that Maia
represents unkind second thoughts on the subject of Hilde and the adequacy
of Youth.

Irene : Now I have risen from the dead. And I sought thee
and found thee. And I see that thou and life lie dead together
—as I have lain. The young woman risen from the dead can
see all life lying on its bier.

Then Rubek seizes her, crying : " Then let us two cold
corpses—this one time only—live life to its depths before we
go down to our graves again." On the heights, in the sunrise, where the powers of light and darkness may look on,
they will stand, he and his bride " restored by grace to me
a sinner ".

It is a vision only. This is what they see. But in a moment
they are overwhelmed by the avalanche and the mist, and
the Deaconess speaks the last word as the Voice had spoken
it in *Brand* : " *Pax vobiscum.*"

The connexions with *Love's Comedy, On the Vidda* and
Brand are unmistakable. What personal renunciation was
behind these works it would be impertinent to know ; but
they are themselves exultant, confident, they seem to greet
a Resurrection Day. The renunciation, whatever it was,
was exhilarating to Ibsen then. There is no need of external
reference to interpret the vision, where the woman of the
Resurrection Day rises again and sees life lying on its bier.
The patterned strictness of *When we Dead Wake* means that
in any case the underlying experience has been modified
profoundly to fit an apocalyptic symbolism. The three acts
are symmetrically arranged—the valley, the hillside, the
heights. Each act consists of a scene between Rubek and
Maia (in the last act, Ulfheim and Maia) followed by one
between Rubek and Irene. Irene, the white-clad ghostly
statue, Maia with her alpenstock and mountain dress, the
savage Ulfheim with his pack of dogs, the black-robed
Deaconess with her cross upon her breast, are like figures on
a frieze. They would not gain by representation. It is clear
that Ibsen did not mean the Dramatic Epilogue to be acted.
To almost every speech, for example, he has added elaborate
stage directions, indicating the tone and gestures to accompany
it : this would be an insult to actors, and Ibsen was far too

great a craftsman to be guilty of it. On the stage of his day the play would in any case be unactable : the second and third acts show open stretches of country and the scene shifts without a curtain while the final avalanche would have defeated the representational producer altogether.

Many of Irene's earlier speeches—in fact almost all the first act—is intelligible only in the light of later passages : this will not do on the stage. The lurid glow of madness which had lit up Solness's speeches also lights up hers. In manner, the play anticipates the more symbolic plays of Strindberg, such as *The Ghost Sonata* (1901). Indeed throughout the later plays there is a flavour of Strindberg, and it will be remembered that Ibsen kept a portrait of Strindberg in his study.[1]

That Ibsen wrote the play in great pain and distress, that he collapsed after writing it, is not surprising, since, if it has any personal significance at all—and this can hardly be disputed—it is a condemnation of all he had written since he turned his back on poetry and Norway. With the inerrant honesty that was his glory and his curse, Ibsen held a last doom-session over himself. It was but fitting that the ending should be heroic and set in a heroic scene, upon the very summit of the western heights.

[1] He said that he liked the diabolic expression in the eyes.

Chapter Six

IBSEN OUR CONTEMPORARY; HIS
DRAMAS ON THE MODERN STAGE

THE scenic pre-eminence of Ibsen has been strikingly re-
asserted on the English stage since the end of the second
world war; he has now become an English classic, to be
performed in the National Theatre. The growing popularity
of the whole range of his plays on the stage and for broad-
casting can be seen by a glance at the appendixes to volumes
V and VI of J. W. McFarlane's Oxford Ibsen (1960). All
the main plays have been regularly revived; even the rare
historical plays have attracted amateurs. Between 1950
and 1952, the entire series of the plays was broadcast by the
B.B.C. In 1960, simultaneously with the Oxford Ibsen, the
publication of an acting version of all the plays was started
by Michael Meyer.

Living theatre has so refashioned this nineteenth-century
writer that he has emerged, in something the same fashion as
Kott's Shakespeare, as "Ibsen our Contemporary" and this
by a like process—the growing impulse of theatrical directors
to handle literary masterpieces with greater freedom and
sophistication. The greatest success has attended his later
plays, those in which Ibsen is nearest to Strindberg. Such
characters as Rosmer, Rebekke, Hedda, Solness and Hilde
have been developed by interpretations based on depth psychology—it has already been noted in an earlier chapter that
The Sea Woman can be played, almost too easily, as something
very like a case history. But depth psychology has led the
modern playwright and producer beyond naturalism to a
new kind of action; in the modern French "Theatre of
Cruelty" (the theatre of Ionesco and Genet, Artaud and
Adamov), actors and audience are together engaged in a
psychodrama which involves extremes of fantasy. This
theatre, in its "magic relation to reality and danger" ' involves
the audience by surrealist techniques, by shocks and by the
release from taboos, rather than by orderly plot or narrative.

In spite of his classic form, Ibsen originally produced a not dissimilar effect by his shocking disregard of convention; he challenged and was even held to have insulted the audience. Modern theatre thrives on insults—on provocation and evocation at a level quite different from the cool and overt intellectual challenges of Ibsen, Brieux or Shaw. Yet Ibsen's plays have proved themselves capable of translation into this modern symbolic theatrical idiom, by virtue of the hidden or covert challenges carried by their suppressed poetry.

In 1955, when Samuel Beckett's *Waiting for Godot* introduced this type of drama effectually to the English stage, a reinterpretation of the English dramatic classics was set going. Current reinterpretations of Shakespeare have sometimes reached very startling lengths; and Ibsen, though less obviously, has been affected by the movement at present centred on the Royal Court and Aldwych Theatres.

Already, at the beginning of the century, when Ibsen's thought was still considered advanced, James Joyce indicated the means by which his works were eventually to escape from the limitations of their age, and from the misconceptions of his early admirers:

> If any plays demand a stage, they are the plays of Ibsen . . . they are so packed with thought. At some chance expression, the mind is tortured with some question, and in a flash, long reaches of life are opened up in vista, yet the vision is momentary unless we stay to ponder it. It is just to prevent excessive pondering that Ibsen requires to be acted.
>
> (*Fortnightly Review*, April 1900).

The spectator himself must not be too analytically and consciously preoccupied with the contents of the play. He is totally engaged, and not merely interested as a thinker or planner. That lonely or buried aspect of Ibsen which speaks through poetic symbols, or through the more primitive "languages" of gesture, grouping and stage objects, springs into action here.

The plays of Ibsen's maturity are characterized by a shift from the fully articulate to the indirect, from poetry in the words to poetry behind the words. McFarlane speaks of his "inner dialogue, those exchanges conducted behind the spoken word, so eloquently inarticulate", observing that *The Wild Duck* is "so ordered as to give an astoundingly successful illusion of perspective in depth"; this, largely through its language, "the loading of it with extra and secretly shared significance, as when Gregers talks to Hedvig".

The loaded quality of the presentation also—of staging and décor—has been investigated by John Northam, who shows how the power of visual suggestion "adds unspoken information, where strict realism inhibits open statement of feeling and motive" and how therefore the production can "help to steer the mind through many situations where dialogue alone presents merely a choice between conflicting interpretations of Character" (*Ibsen's Dramatic Method*, Faber, 1952, p. 12). By a stage setting with some flowers, a shawl, a lamp, or by some careful stage direction, Ibsen builds emotional responses into his play, that are never overtly part of what is being said in the dialogue.

Sometimes, in this way, he can achieve great richness and complexity of feeling—fusions that would not be possible in the more precise, more defined medium of words. For example, in *Rosmersholm*, I think that the white shawl which Rebekke is crocheting throughout the play, and which she wears to her death is not merely, as Dr. Northam suggests, a shroud, whose colour connects it with the White Horses that are the forms of the returning dead. It is also her bridal veil, for her death is at the same time her wedding to Rosmer ; the White Horses, symbols of death, are also universal symbols of life and energy ; and the white waters of the mill race turn the wheels that grind the corn, as well as receiving on their tossing foam the bodies of the two sacrificial victims. Here is a paradox and a contradiction ; the waters of life and death flow mingled together in the terror and exaltation that the tragedy sets free. Such a paradox, to be stated in words, would demand poetry of the most concentrated sort.

So, therefore, although the social challenge of Rosmer and Rebekke no longer makes an appeal in the intellectual terms that once it carried, something of the same effect may be gained more obscurely through the action of symbols on the modern stage.   Only the most imaginative and dramatically sophisticated reader, however, is likely to be able to create this effect for himself by reading the text.   It demands to be seen.

Had Ibsen written in a language more generally understood, had he been able to rely on close verbal texture and poetic intensity, his peculiar ability for *dramatic* statement, for " the words behind the words " might not have developed as it did.   His initial difficulties in communicating to the theatre of his exile evoked in him that kind of theatrical language which loses the minimum by translation ; and also developed the more primitive " languages " of gesture, colour, grouping, which do not need translation at all.   His masterly construction, which ensures that so much goes unstated, is partly dependent on the qualities of his original language, as I have already explained in Chapter I.   Yet again—by a strange chance—his particular situation, though exceptional in his own day, corresponds to one which is now much more universal.

The rapidity of social changes in our time, and the failure of language to keep up with these changes, mean that the loneliness and lack of communication, the isolation that gave so unusual a strength and ironic concentration to Ibsen, have now become a common condition of the artist, and indeed of the ordinary man.   Ibsen, as an exile, anticipated the self-chosen lot of many modern poets—from Eliot and Auden to Thom Gunn, who all chose exile.

> Now it is fog, I walk
> Contained within my coat
> No castle more cut off
> By reason of its moat :
> Only the sentry's cough,
> The mercenaries' talk.

The street lamps, visible,
Drop no light on the ground,
But press beams painfully
In a yard of fog around.
I am condemned to be
An individual.

Thom Gunn, *Human Condition.*

To state such loneliness, is by implication to transcend it ; yet the exceptional strain involved for one who is " condemned to be an individual " is not made less thereby.   Therefore the drama, because of its appeal to deeper and more primitive levels of impulse, to simpler and more instinctive modes of expression, with its power to unite these primitive feelings to the difficult level of articulated thought, has now become the favourite medium of the artist in words.   More than the novel, more than the lyric, the drama speaks to our human condition because it can make use of a much wider variety of " languages ", for a much more complex range of integrative material ; it can also unite the separate individuals through their common participation in this social art.

The heir of James Joyce is Samuel Beckett ; and in Beckett's plays, as in the plays of Ardern, Pinter and others, poetic imagination uses a speech which is deliberately inadequate. As Ibsen had done, these writers present much of what they have to say in terms of stage production and of settings. The attic of *The Wild Duck* may be compared with the refuge of Hamm and Clov in *Endgame*, or Nora's doll's house with the sandhill of *Happy Days*, in which the heroine is buried first up to her waist and then up to her neck. In Pinter, as in Ibsen, many characters are deeply inarticulate ; so that dialogue apparently flat or trivial becomes loaded with implication which the audience and actors supply.   The hero and his tormentors in *The Birthday Party* depend upon " exchanges behind the spoken word, so eloquently inarticulate ", if no longer in quite the way that Ibsen's characters did. Pinter's appeal to deeper levels, which is the result of greater modern sophistication and insight into the workings of the mind, has shifted the emphasis in the modern theatre towards what is indirectly suggested ; it has decreased the weight placed on dialogue, in favour of what may be deduced from it. And this brings both actors and audiences into necessary collaboration.

This movement towards the activity of the theatre restores to Ibsen's plays the force which was originally theirs by reason of his handling of disturbing social problems. But in addition, the very feelings of distance which are now confessed by his nineteenth-century settings and idiom, by all that belongs to the past, may act as filters, helping to adjust the audience to the right measure of detachment and judgment, in spite of the direct force of the theatre. In a great play, the audience and actors must be drawn in ; but they must also and simultaneously be given a measure of freedom, and even of " alienation ".

For this purpose, certain modern playwrights will set their plays in the past rather than the present, as Brecht did in *The Life of Galileo*, Sartre in *Lucifer and the Lord*, and Camus in *The Just*. The classical form of such writers brings them closer to Ibsen than is the " Theatre of Cruelty ", yet I think it is the stage techniques of the latter group which have been chiefly responsible for the dramatic revolution of the past decade. Now every playwright has vine leaves in his hair.

Ibsen's own earlier and more Dionysiac play of *Peer Gynt* lends itself to staging by contemporary techniques ; the madhouse scene can be played as virtually a miniature version of Peter Weiss's *Murder of Marat*. Thanks to the modern resources of the theatre, both *Peer Gynt* and *Brand* can become live drama in a sense that would have been impossible in Ibsen's own day.

A reader may be helped to elicit the poetic core of the later plays by the help of Ibsen's early lyrics. Some of these, which as poetry are not remarkable, have already been discussed in Chapter II ; and translations of a number are now given in an appendix. It will be noticed in how many of them images of wounded, crazed, or tortured wild creatures appear (and there are others about caged birds etc.). The power of these

images to suggest the vulnerable core of the individual human
being, his inarticulate animal suffering, is often made explicit
in simile or comment.

Ibsen's close relation with Norway—which has been the
main subject of this book—is no more of a handicap to a
modern audience than the now distant social and intellectual
problems with which Ibsen worked. For there is a general
impulse to compensate in art for the rootlessness and im-
personality of the modern city, the chain of identical air
terminals and associated hotels which circles the earth. Plays
which involve an environment, such as the North of England
or the American South, exert a special appeal even on those
who may have no acquaintance with the region in question ;
therefore the domesticity of Ibsen's Norway, which he so
detested but could never escape from, becomes now an asset
rather than a limitation.

None the less, Ibsen was the first dramatist to set out the
life of the modern city dweller as theme of a tragic play. It is
paradoxical that the writer who first saw the dramatic poten-
tiality that lay in the lives of bank clerks and photographers
should belong to the least urbanized country of Western
Europe. Although, in common with every other nation,
Norway is now experiencing a drift to the towns, her capital
city still numbers under half a million inhabitants, scattered
round the arms of the great Oslo Fjord, while Bergen (Norway's second city) contains only 120,000 people. Drama, as
Yeats observed, is essentially of the city ; it has flourished best
in the capitals of Athens, London, Paris, Berlin, Moscow.

So, in turning to drama, Ibsen went clean contrary to the
literary bent of his own people, which is essentially bardic
or narrative. In the little scattered villages or the upland farms
of a rural community, literature tends to the lyric or to the
tale. This remains still true of Norway—though, for example,
it is no longer true of Ireland. At the Bergen National Theatre,
where Ibsen began his career in 1852, I have seen Eugène
O'Neill produced with all the characters symmetrically
grouped (turned half or full to the footlights) and, for most

of the act, seated round a large central table, in the manner of Victorian family photographs. I have heard the audience laughing delightedly at more obvious jokes, but clearly unprepared for anything disturbing or demanding. It was not only the lace tippets of the elderly *bourgeoises* that remained from Ibsen's time, almost unchanged.

In the land of his birth, Ibsen is still treated with a certain reserve. Although the history of his theatrical productions is at present the subject of an investigation at the University of Oslo, the Ibsen that is recognized at home is the now long-deceased inhabitant of a heavily upholstered study, or the formidable old autocrat who, after setting his watch by the University clock, walked each day down Karl Johansgate, to his morning coffee in the palm-decked Grand Café. For the English student of drama he has grown an altogether more demoniac figure, dealing in primitive sacrifices, in dark cults that contrast strangely with his surface decorum and brilliant technique. Like some explorer with finely tuned instruments and equipment of the utmost scientific precision, Ibsen advances into the interior jungle, the darkness that lies within the single individual, the wild places of the human spirit.

The renewed theatrical life that Ibsen enjoys has elicited many new translations of his plays. In addition to the two complete translations which have been started, a number of writers have essayed one or more plays, and in all of these a direct and vivid colloquial speech has been striven for. Some of the new versions (like James Forsyth's verse rendering of *Brand*) are extremely free ; but one or two are almost as literal as Archer's. By an irony that might have amused Ibsen, his own Norwegian speech has now become so out of date that there is talk of translating him into one of the many modern versions of his own language—Nynorsk, or the later hybrid form, which combines this with Riksmål. So that eventually, he may survive *only* in translation.

To the English translator, Ibsen presents a variety of problems. There are many phrases which call for no special skill, being of the very bone and nerve of all drama—phrases such as Judge Brack's " People don't do such things ! " or Hjalmer's despairing " No, no, she *must* live ". But a comparison of various interpretations of the closing words of *The Wild Duck* will shew how much legitimate variation is possible. Archer's version runs :

> *Relling :* Oh, life would be quite tolerable after all, if only we could get rid of the confounded duns that keep on pestering us, in our poverty, with the claim of the ideal.
> *Gregers* (looking straight before him) : In that case, I am glad my destiny is what it is.
> *Relling :* May I enquire, what is your destiny ?
> *Gregers* (going) : To be the thirteenth at table.
> *Relling :* The devil it is.

McFarlane renders the same passage :

> *Relling :* Oh, life wouldn't be too bad if only these blessed people who come canvassing their ideals round everybody's door would leave us poor souls in peace.
> *Gregers* (staring into space) : In that case I am glad my destiny is what it is.
> *Relling :* If I may ask—what is your destiny ?
> *Gregers* (turning to leave) : To be the thirteenth at table.
> *Relling :* The devil it is !

Relling's first speech is beautifully adapted by McFarlane for stage speaking ; and his stage directions also are written for the actors, being more precise than Archer's. The latest translation (Rolf Fjelde's) reads :

> *Relling :* Oh, life would be good, in spite of all, if we could only have some peace from those damned shysters who come badgering us poor people with their " summons to the ideal ".
> *Gregers* (staring straight ahead) : In that case, I'm glad my destiny is what it is.
> *Relling :* Beg pardon—but what *is* your destiny ?
> *Gregers* (about to leave) : To be the thirteenth at the table.
> *Relling :* Oh, the hell you say.

This last exclamation, which Farquherson Sharp renders
' So I should imagine ' and Una Ellis-Fermor ' I wonder. . . .'
seems to make a weak curtain line.   I should like to give it
a slightly different twist, which depends on Gregers's view of
his " bestemmelse ", the word which everyone translates
" destiny ".   This word can also mean simply " destination ";
and in that moment when he " stares into space ", I think
Gregers should appear to see a path, something like a ship's
course, along which he moves slowly off in a tranced way,
as Macbeth follows the air-drawn dagger.   To be thirteenth
at table means death, and I think his words indicate that he is
following the path on which he had set the little sister with
whom he enjoyed such deep instinctive sympathy.   The way
he moves off should be sufficient to show that he is acting
with the kind of automatism that Julie displays at the end of
Strindberg's play.   The intention is made much clearer in
the early draft of this scene (given both by Archer and
McFarlane):

Relling : Do you think it's so important then that life should
be lived ?
Gregers : I don't.   On the contrary.   But my fate isn't to live
my life either, I have another mission.
Relling : What mission is that ?
Gregers : To be thirteenth at table (he goes).
Relling : The devil it is.

Ibsen has added Relling's outburst, only to precipitate
Gregers's despair.   The final moment belongs to Gregers as
an actor, but with these varying tones and moods, implied
by his ironic questions and his final exclamation, it is Relling's
speeches that tax the translator.   Although the last line has
been translated sometimes as mere musing, sometimes as
scorn, and sometimes as surprised acceptance, I would like
to think that Relling is meant to gain a sudden insight into
what he proposes to do by Gregers's tone and movement ;
and that he acknowledges it.   So that I would like some such
words as " What the devil, I believe you're right ! " to end
the play.   Gregers, the despairing idealist, like Julie is given

the Order of Release, from his cynical but clear-sighted companion ; Relling's final lines recognizes that he can provide no " life-lie ", no saving fantasy, for Gregers, who is therefore given the only form of support that the doctor can now supply. The examination of such a passage serves to shew that close reading can still extract new meanings from Ibsen, such as are characteristic of poetry rather than of prose. It is the poetic quality of his imagination which offers, to the actor and to the attentive reader alike, an opportunity to enter the work and re-live it from within ; thus, by an ever-renewed act of creation, making it into something that is reborn with each occasion.

The power of generating new and valid imaginative experience is the cause of Ibsen's continuing stage success. It has been suggested that this is due to those qualities which his relative linguistic isolation forced upon him, and which correspond to the common situation of the artist at the present day. Hence those hardships and challenges which circumstances imposed have proved the means to ensure that his work survives with reputation as great as ever, if indeed it has not been enhanced in the course of the century that has now elapsed since, in 1864, he quitted Norway for Italy and fame.

APPENDIX

Twelve Poems from Ibsen

The first eight poems are included for their relation to particular plays ; the last four as autobiographical confessions.

I

The Vision of the High Fjells
(Originally written for a *tableau vivant*; compare *Peer Gynt*)

The dales lie in the summer night
Under long shadows, blind;
A tossing sea surrounds the height
Driven by the evening wind.
There the cloud-waves welter grey;
No more the sight can rest
On the high glacier which, by day,
Looks out to dwellings far away
With sungold on its crest.

But in the mist of waves afire,—
Gold-splendour and ambergreece—
The crags through this far sea pierce higher,
A realm of joy and peace,
The great gier-eagle sailing by
Like a ship far, far abroad;
Beyond, in sable panoply,
The trolls' array stands threateningly
Turned to the West and God.

Dark 'neath the glacier's pendant rim,
Cowshed and cheese-hut hide;
Snows glittering-white, heights purple-dim
Surround it far and wide.
The dwellers in that quiet home
Remote 'mid rock and streams,
Know heaven as a more spacious dome,
Friended by warmer beams.

The saeter girl in silence stays
With glow and shadow barred;

The earnest charm that holds her gaze
No veil of words has blurred.
She knows not where she would aspire,
What name the place may bear—
But from the glacier and the byre
Launches into the sunset's fire—
Does she find harbour there?

The mountain life alas, how brief
In the saeter under the scree.
Soon in a snow cloak folded stiff
Will cowshed and cheese-hut lie.
Then by the stove sit down and hold
Your wonted winter ways,
Your wool to spin and hemp to fold—
One vision of sunset's mountain gold
This winter life repays.

II

The Miner

(Compare *John Gabriel Borkman*)

Tunnel, burst with boom and crash
Before my hammer's heavy smash!
Deeper still my way I bore,
Till I hear the ring of ore.

Deep within the hill's waste night
Treasures beckon rich and bright,
Diamonds and precious gems,
Amid the gold-vein's branching stems.

And in the depth below is peace,
That was, and is, and shall not cease.
Burst my way, then, heavy hammer,
To the heart's deep-hidden chamber!

Once, a lad, I too was gay
Under heaven's star-ranked array ;
I trod the springtime's flowery ways,
And bore a child's peace in my gaze.

Day's splendour I no more recall
Under the midnight's murky pall,
Nor song nor rustle of the trees
Within my temple's cavities.

When to these depths I first was brought
" The spirits of the deep " I thought
In innocence, " shall answer give
To the blank riddle, how to live ".

Not a spirit will reveal
What so sorely I must feel ;
Ne'er a gleam of light around,
Ne'er a glow from underground.

Have I failed, to follow here
This way on towards the Clear ?
Rays will blind my dazzled eyes,
If to the heights I seek to rise.

No, in the deep, down must I bore.
There is peace for evermore.
Burst my way then, heavy hammer,
To the heart's deep-hidden chamber !

Blow on hammer-blow I shower
To my lifetime's final hour,
Without a single streak of morning,
Without the achievement of the dawning.

M

III

The Stormy Petrel

(Compare *The Wild Duck*)

Where the Petrel breeds, landfall is far to seek—
So I heard an old sea captain speak.

The blind driving spray on her wings is blown;
She sinks not, but treads the long rollers down.

With the sea down she sinks: with the sea does she rise:
In dead calm she's mute: in the storm she cries.

Half-flying, half-swimming she weathers the swell,
As dreamers touch heaven, are cast into hell.

Too light for the billow, too heavy for air—
Bird-winged words of the poet, our sorrow is there!

Yes, and the worst is—in clever men's eyes,
Most of it's only an old salt's lies....

IV

The Eider Duck

(Compare *The Wild Duck*

The Eider-duck breeds by Norway's shore;
He haunts the edge of the blue grey fjord.

He tears from his bleeding breast the down,
To build his nest both soft and warm.

But the fjordside fisherman, savage churl,
Plunders the nest to the last soft curl.

The fisher is hard, yet the bird lives warm ,
For again he will pluck his breast of down.

And, plundered again, he will build in a cleft,
And line the nest with the feathers left.

But rob him thrice, of his last poor mite,
He spreads his wings to the young spring night,

Breasts the mist bleeding and sheers in a run
To the South, to the South, to the coasts of the Sun !

V

Mind's-Might
(Compare Ulfheim in *When We Dead Awaken*)

Hear how an animal-tamer will set
Out to teach a led bear what it shall not forget.

In a brewer's kettle he binds the brute,
Sets kindling under, and puts fire to 't.

Meanwhile he plays a jolly air,
" Enjoy your life ! " to the roasting bear.

Pain fuses the brute's feelings all to a lump—
He cannot stand, he must dance and jump.

Henceforth if that melody ever is played him,
He feels a dancing devil invade him.

I myself in the vat once found a seat,
With full orchestra and pretty good heat.

That time I singed rather more than my hide,
And the memory will not be laid aside.

So now if an echo of those days I feel,
It's as if I were laid upon glowing steel.

As a stab to the root of the nail it will pierce—
Straightway I must dance on the feet of a verse.

VI

Blue Print

(Compare *Bygmester Solness*)

That night when in print I first saw my verse appear !
As if it were but yesterday it stands out sharp and clear.
In my poor little sanctum, clouded in tobacco haze,
There I sat, adreaming, puffing, drunk with glory and self praise.

" I'll build a castle in the clouds shall rule the Northern sky,
With a Great Hall and a Lesser Hall blazing brilliantly :
The Great Hall shall give shelter to Norway's Hero-Bard,
The Lesser Hall do service youthful maidenhood to guard".

Thought and object were most strikingly concordant !   Later though,
The Master gaining sanity, discord began to grow
In the lunatic sky castle—the Great Hall dwindled, shrunk,
While the Lesser Hall, disintegrate, in shapeless ruin sunk.

VII

With a Water Lily

(Compare Asta in *Little Eyolf*)

See, beloved, what I bring :
The flower with the pure white wing,
Borne upon the quiet stream,
Swimming in a springtide dream.

Would you give it fitting rest,
Beloved, wear it at your breast.
There the leaves will rest above
Deep waters sliding still and smooth.

Child, beware the tarn-fed stream:
Deadly, deadly, there to dream:
In feigned sleep Nekken lurks below,
Overhead the lilies grow.

Child, thy breast's a tarn-fed stream:
Deadly, deadly there to dream:
Overhead the lilies grow,
In feigned sleep Nekken lurks below.

VIII

Burnt Ships

He turned his prow,
And steered from the North
Seeking lighter gods,
He ventured forth.

The beacons of Snow-land
In the sea sank wavering,
The lure of the Sun-Coast
Calmed all his craving.

He burnt his ships;
The smoke blue-black
Like a cloud-bridge streamed
North-wards and back.

To the huts of the Snow-land
From the Sun-Coast bright
A lonely horseman
Rides north each night.

IX

To my Friend, the Revolutionary Orator

You say, with the Tories is where I belong.
I am what I have been my whole life long.

I won't accept change that shifts brick by brick—
Knock down the house and I'll join you quick.

There's only one revolution I know of
That didn't in action decline and go off.

The first and most glorious—it's understood,
Naturally, that I refer to the Flood.

Yet even then Lucifer missed his effect—
Noah seized the dictatorship, you'll recollect.

Let us set to work as radicals, then !
It needs thought and action, the tongue and the pen.

You flood the world to its high water mark,
And I'll be delighted to sink you the Ark.

X

Portrait of the Artist at Home

The house was still, the street seemed dead,
The lamp where I sat was shrouded,
The room in deep shade was enveloped,
As the children came, greeting with nodded head[1]
Me in Havana-smoke clouded.

[1] A nod is a polite form of greeting in Norway. No words are needed !

My wingèd children again are here,
Lively lasses and lads in legions !
Cheeks as after a bath glowed clear—
Hey presto ! how wild and glad we career
Through all the delightful regions !

But, just as the game was at its best,
I chanced to look in the mirror.
There stood a steady and sober guest,
With steel-grey eyes and close-buttoned vest,
And felt slippers, or I'm in error.

Then fell a weight on my lively rout.
Thumb stuck in mouth, one stares.
Another stands, a lumpish lout,
For the pertest lad, as you know, is put out
If a stranger appears unawares. . . .

XI

The Kirk

With toil wrought the King
Through the daylight's hours :
Under night's dark wing
Pick and crowbar ring,
Wielded by dark powers.

Rose the spire-crowned kirk
In its arrowy pride :
'Neath the royal work
Worming trolls still lurk—
They wrought side by side.

Sunlit or benighted
There were crowds, 'tis true :
The bright day unblighted
To the dark was united—
They were one, not two.

XII

Stars in Nebulae

My comet-track steered in a line
Through empty space in search of home,
Which regions saw a stranger come,
Unlooked-for guest of Andromeda's sign.

Word-bearer down to our ancient earth
From out the high silences afar ;
Where Chaos crystallized into a star
The Law of Cohesion had given it birth.

An unformed mass whirled round in my mind,
With scattered forces, paths that diverged ;
No magnetic impulse an orbit urged,
Nor drove me the central peace to find.

But when I stood out in the silence afar,
I weighed up all that had come to be,
I weighed up what I myself could see—
The light-mist coiling, and shrunk to a star.

I had faith in my light-mist's shapeless blaze,
Unformed, sweeping North on a lawless course ;
I believed in the law of Cohesion's force,
And the lustrous planet's steady rays.

INDEX

Except for the plays of Ibsen and Shakespeare, works are entered under their authors.

171